AF487181

PROCTOLOGY

a bottom examination

Simon Dunn

Copyright © 2022 Simon Dunn

All rights reserved

No part of this book may be reproduced, or stored in a retrieval system, or transmitted in any form or by any means, electronic, mechanical, photocopying, recording, or otherwise, without express written permission of the publisher.

Cover design by: Simon Dunn

for Gusty O'Windflap

CONTENTS

Title Page

Copyright

Dedication

Front   1

Note   6

Passage   8

Line   89

Smells   94

Gas   107

Contest   114

Apocalypse   122

'S Up   130

Accident   137

Digger   144

Culture   152

Burglary   158

Parade   162

Holy   168

'S Out   173

Bottom: Live   177

Hole   193

Terror   200

Break   205

Dough   210

Finger   215

Carnival   220

Bottom Live: The Big Number 2 Tour   225

Bottom Live 3: Hooligan's Island   237

Guest House Paradiso   249

Bottom 2001: An Arse Oddity   261

Bottom Live 2003: Weapons Grade Y-Fronts   268
Tour

Back   277

FRONT

It was a Wednesday break time at school, near the start of term in 1991. I rushed to catch up with a friend, and excitedly asked him if he'd seen *Bottom* last night.

'It was a bit rude,' he said.

That struck me as a rather odd comment, and I replied that it made me laugh so much it hurt. But that was the end of the conversation.

Bottom had arrived with seemingly little fanfare. I may have a seen a trailer for it during some continuity, but to my mind, I think I just sat down to watch it out of habit, because Tuesdays at 9pm on BBC Two usually meant some good comedy. *Rab C Nesbitt* had ended the week before.

I remember thinking as it started 'wow, Rik and Ade have made something new'. (I hadn't seen any of the Dangerous Brothers, and wasn't even aware of *Filthy Rich And Catflap* at the time). And from those opening titles, which conveyed so much melancholy, so much dreary existentialism, so much cartoon violence, and just so much bloody fun, I was hooked. It occurs to me that I recorded it on VHS, so I must have had some advance warning to have had it cued up ready to go. And that tape got watched a lot over the next few years.

The bleak music, the world going on around and in spite of our hapless main characters, and the sheer drabness of it all leant itself to that title.

Bottom.

These two are there. Rock bottom, with nowhere else to go, and no-one else to be with.

The opening scene rockets along, moving us from the front door, in an unusual hand-held shot, along the hall, and into the drawing room (I don't think I've been in there). Rik's clearly enjoying himself, he nearly corpses on a line about clenching his buttocks. The theme of the show unfolds over this long, opening scene, and it's well-stated, and funny throughout. This is a skewering of toxic masculinity and male entitlement at a time when Laddism was about to rise.

To see so much depth in what's essentially a live-action cartoon might seem a little pretentious, but that's the beauty of *Bottom*. Amongst all the mayhem, somewhere in the violence and the bawdy and tawdry shenanigans, there's a melancholic humanity to it. An existential dread. Death is coming, and all we can do about it is sit and watch the telly.

But that's ok, if every week for the next five weeks, I can sit and watch this.

I've never understood the easy dismissal of *Bottom*, even in puff pieces about Rik and Ade.

'The secret of Bottom's huge success is as

(BOTTOM COMES TOP, NEIL HORNE, ABERDEEN
EVENING EXPRESS, 29TH APRIL 1993)

It would be easy to argue that there's so much more to the show than the double-entendres and the violence. But that undervalues some brilliant writing, and completely dismisses some of the best slapstick comedy sequences ever committed to screen. The fight at the end of *Culture* is at once hilarious, and completely earned in the story, with everything before-hand building into the frustration and boredom that finally erupts into violence. These bottle episodes, with just Richie and Eddie stuck together in the flat are *Bottom* at its finest, and every bit as good as anything that influenced it, be it Beckett, Tati, or Hancock, or *Steptoe And Son*.

Bottom may be the culmination of the characters they've been playing since *20th Century Coyote*, through Rick and Vyvyan, The Dangerous Brothers, and *Filthy, Rich And Catflap*, but by the time we reach the Hammersmith Hooligans (I wonder how much that grotty flat is worth now), there's an added depth to their world, an almost antediluvian satire.

Like *The Young Ones*, which isn't of its time, rather than being ABOUT its time, so is *Bottom*. The rage-fuelled punk reaction to the cruelties of Thatcherism has given way to the seething apathy to the growing sleaze, corruption, and the wilful distraction of the early stirrings of the Back To Basics philosophy of Majorism.

'The old values – neighbourliness, decency, courtesy – they're still alive, they're still the best of Britain.' A phrase that could easily have come from Richie's mouth as it did from John Major's.

It's about middle-aged impotence – in more ways than one. That youthful rage was all for nought. Thatcher survived a decade, and gave way to something just as insidious, and all their anger did nothing to change that.

(When the country regained its collective hope (justified or not), Richie and Eddie couldn't be allowed that hope. For them, things couldn't only get better. They're cruelly stranded on a desert island.)

Everything about *Bottom* is old, and dilapidated, just like the United Kingdom had become under the Tories in the preceding decade. A decaying monument to the past. And here, two of the biggest victims of it all, hark back to a time that never even existed. They get up every morning and put on a suit and tie, even though they've nowhere to go. They wear their hats to the pub, and talk wistfully about an England that's just a myth, using arcane swear-words, conjuring up images of cricket, vicars, teas on the lawn. The sense of white male entitlement is palpable.

But then, in horrible moments of self-realisation, they realise their place in the world.

'I think I've reached my bottom.'

Richie and Eddie aren't even the heroes of their own story.

While other 90s shows embraced laddism, *Bottom* somehow managed to pre-empt all that. Contrast Tony and Gary in *Men Behaving Badly*, who never quite get their comeuppance, with Richie and Eddie, who are clearly the butt of the joke – no-one likes them, they don't even like each other, and no matter what, at the end of each and every episode, they get squarely kicked in the knackers.

And the world keeps on kicking them in the knackers. Over and over again.

It's relentlessly bleak, it's a post-Thatcher tirade, and it's bloody hilarious.

NOTE

This guide is divided into a few different sections. Passage explores the public and professional works of Rik and Ade from when they met at University right up to the first broadcast of *Smells*. It is not, nor is it meant to be, exhaustive, and examines works that fed into the creation of *Bottom*.

Most of the newspaper clippings were found on the *British Newspaper Archive*, and many of the magazine articles are available in high quality digital scans from the fabulous '*Rik Mayall Scrapbook*' website. Lots of the TV clips that haven't been released commercially can be seen on the excellent '*Rik Mayall – The Legend*' YouTube channel.

Line gives a quick overview of the *Bottom* production, broadcast, and live show schedule.

The episodes are presented in original broadcast order (with the exception of '*S Out*). Each entry begins with credits, recording and transmission details, BARB ratings (overall/channel), a listings blurb from the day of broadcast, and a synopsis. The Guff section is my thoughts as I re-watched each show, and the Nuggets section is a collection of trivia and other observations.

The live shows, and *Guest House Paradiso* are explored in chronological order, and are split into similar sections as the episodes of the sitcom.

PASSAGE

1976

A year after Margaret Thatcher assumed leadership of the Conservative party, there was a small advert in *The Stage* on the 25th November, 1976. It probably seemed rather innocuous at the time, and no-one could have known its importance in the development of what became Alternative Comedy.

> *'Notice is hereby given that Lloyd Peters ... carrying on business under the name of '20th Century Coyote' intends to apply to the Manchester City Council for registration under the above act.'*

Peters was studying Drama at Manchester University, and he began this improv troupe, along with his housemate Rik Mayall, and a few other students in their year (Mark Dewison and Mike Redfearn), and Adrian Edmondson. They would soon become the resident players at The Band On The Wall, a music venue in the Northern Quarter of Manchester.

'We used to pass the hat round at the end, and we kind of got a reputation for being take-the-piss nuisances really. And we kind of revelled in that.' So said Rik in an interview in 1993.

Coyote developed out of a Monday evening Manchester University drama department initiative called *Studio Night*.

> *'You'd get up and do anything you wanted in front of the whole department. That's when Rik and I started doing our stuff really. Could be two minutes long or 10 minutes. You'd have a £10 budget from the department. We once bought a couple of pink duvet covers - our plan was to hang them up from the ceiling and be god's testicles. But they wouldn't hold our weight.'*

(ADRIAN EDMONDSON WEBCHAT, THE GUARDIAN,11TH OCTOBER 2017)

According to Rik, in *The Rik Mayall: Bigger Than Hitler, Better Than Christ*, they soon ventured out into pubs in Manchester, performing under various names like *Deathsquad Theatre Company*, and of course Coyote.

1979

The troupe's first show was called *Dead Funny*, and they did six more different shows, before heading for the Edinburgh Fringe. By December of 1979, Thatcher was now Prime Minister (her

Government had slashed taxes for the rich and was preparing to sell off nationalised assets), and Coyote's latest show, *The Wart*, was touring the country. It was even announced in *The Stage*.

> *'20th Century Coyote is presenting 'The Wart' at Theatremarket ... and later at Hoxton Hall, Abbey Centre and Theatrespace. In the company are Barbara Mackie, Nick Hamm, Rick Mayall [sic], Ade Edmondson and Steve Green.'*

At the end of the month, a review of *The Wart* appeared in *The Stage*, part of which focuses on the Beckett parody that formed a big chunk of the show.

> *'Through the Beckett parody, though, there shines more than a hint of respect, as the two performers ... are themselves tatty vaudeville clowns in the Vladimir and Estragon tradition. Mayall is the more dominant of the two, with Edmondson the unselfish foil, timing his feed lines to perfection. Both are razor sharp, versatile and above all, unpredictable, never settling for the easy laugh.'*

Around the same time, Mayall and Edmondson were performing alone as a double-act. In August of 1979, the financial success of their Edinburgh show *Death On The Toilet* ('I played Death and God and Ade played Edwin, the guy it all happened to.' (Oh That Rik Mayall, Sunday Times, 20th March 1983)) encouraged the pair to head for London to stage their new show *King Ron And His Nubile Daughter*.

> *'The whole thing was a disaster. We played twelve different venues ... and attracted an audience of eight people. That's true that.'*

(THE RIK MAYALL, PG 48)

Mayall goes on to say that one show at the Tramshed in Woolwich attracted a reviewer from The Times, who described him as a 'very talented young maniac'.

He was certainly getting noticed. Just the year before Rik had toured America with the *Oxford And Cambridge Shakespeare Company*, who found him via the *National Student Drama Festival* in York (where he won the Boris Karloff Award for Most Outrageous Ham). He played Dromio in *The Comedy Of Errors*, which was co-directed by Jon Plowman.

> *'He was brilliant upon first meeting. A combination of nervous energy and ferocious comic ability, a must-have even then. Onstage, he fascinated both the eye and the mind, and invented comic business as though he'd been doing it for years ... He was also irritatingly good-looking.'*

(HOW TO PRODUCE COMEDY BRONZE, JON PLOWMAN, PG 156)

Rik accidentally broke Jon's arm, a story Jon

recounts in his book, and one Rik writes about like this:

> *'Note to editor: I'll right some stuff ... about when I went to America ... I can mention ... police car chases, drugs ... helicopter incidents, speedboat getaways, shout outs with real guns, explosives, breaking Jon Plowman's arm etc. Don't worry, it'll be great.'*

(THE RIK MAYALL, PG 46)

Rik also appeared as Seyton in *Macbeth* on stage during April of 1980, and made his debut on TV screens as 1st Supporter on the 1st October in Thames Television's *The Squad*.

Back in London at the end of the seventies, Rik learned of the Comedy Store, and went along to watch. It was situated in the upper room of The Gargoyle on Dean Street, which usually played host to *The Nell Gwynne Revue*. But at 10pm, the strippers gave way to the comedians. Rik performed solo, as well as with Ade, honing their act alongside *The Outer Limits* (Peter Richardson and Nigel Planer) and Alexei Sayle.

Looking for more opportunities, Richardson went across the road to the Paul Raymond Revue, and started *The Comic Strip*, so they could all perform six nights a week. They were soon joined by French and Saunders, and TV producers started to take notice.

1980

Among them was Paul Jackson, who pitched a 26 episode cabaret series to the BBC, who loved the idea so much that they commissioned a single episode. *Boom Boom ... Out Go The Lights* was broadcast on the 14 October 1980, and featured a host of solo acts, including Rik playing Rick The Poet, and Nigel Planer as Neil.

Jackson's choice to not showcase the double acts meant Ade and Richardson did not appear, and marked the beginning of a long running feud between the producer and the other half of the *Outer Limits*. Viewers tuning in to BBC Two that night at 10.20pm were also treated to Alexei Sayle singing *Ullo John, Gotta New Motor?*.

Throughout the year, Thatcher's government had already halved state benefits to striking workers, and raised duty on petrol, alcohol, and tobacco. Riots erupted in Bristol, British Aerospace was sold off, the SAS stormed the Iranian Embassy, and unemployment reached a post-war high of two million.

All this was going on as Rik popped up on *Friday Night, Saturday Morning* on 31st October, while a review of *The Comic Strip* live revue appeared, in of all places, the *Bedfordshire on Sunday*.

> 'The stars of the evening were a duo called
> 20th Century Coyote. Rik Mayall and Adrian

Edmondson have the foetus of one of the funniest acts I've ever seen. They satirise playwright Samuel Beckett in one breath and rock and roll singer Gene Vincent in the next.'

(JEFF KATZ, BEDFORDSHIRE ON SUNDAY, 30TH NOVEMBER 1980)

1981

At the start of 1981, BBC Two began airing the *Oxford Road Show*, which may have served as the inspiration for *Nozin' Aroun'* on *The Young Ones*. It was filmed at Broadcasting House on the Oxford Road in Manchester, and was announced in *The Stage* like this.

> *'A new BBC Manchester magazine series, which takes a lighter look at the week's news, is to start on BBC-2 on Friday January 16 at 7.0pm ... Producer of the 11 week series is David Geen and the presenters are Rik Mayall and Rob Rohrer.'*

(THE STAGE, 2ND JANUARY 1981)

The Belfast Telegraph, on the day of the first show, said that 'the aim is to have a lucid look at topical and timely subjects with Rik, who is 23, peppering in song, dance and humour and Rob, with the journalistic background, adding a dash of information and illustration – the audience get their say too.'

Rik never did present the show, and while it's

speculation, it is possible he shot a non-broadcast pilot and it was decided to replace him with guest co-presenters like Martin Bergman or Jackie Spreckley. It's also possible that Rik dropped out to film his part in the *Rocky Horror Picture Show* sequel *Shock Treatment* which was in production around this time.

Ben Elton did make a few appearances on the *Oxford Road Show*, albeit in more languid (and possibly bored and/or fed up) form than on his later *Saturday Live* hosting duties. *20th Century Coyote* performed on the show at the start of the second series in November of 1981. They also appeared on the late night BBC Two show *Friday Night, Saturday Morning* on 30th January, and again on 6th March.

In May that year, a second episode of *Boom Boom* was broadcast, and this time Ade appeared with Rik as The Dangerous Brothers. They adapted their language here too, swapping out some expletives for the more arcane 'plopping', a technique that carried right through to *Bottom*.

An unexpurgated version of this same Dangerous Brothers routine appears in *The Comic Strip*, a 1981 short film directed by Julien Temple. In September of 1981 the *Comic Strip* recorded an album, for the Springtime! Label, and released it in October.

> *'The Comic Strip is a sleazy dive for trend-*
> *setting humourists, home of the new wave*
> *comedians ... This album, recorded in Paul*

The album was received with some controversy, mainly for the language, and three major stockists (Boots, Woolworths and WH Smith) refused to sell it. An advertising campaign was cancelled by London Transport, after only appearing on a few red buses.

In that same edition of the paper, there's an article announcing the replacement of *The Comic Strip* at the Boulevard Theatre, promising more material turnover, and called *The Comedy Cabaret*. Run by Andrew de la Tour. It ran twice nightly on Fridays and Saturdays, and was compered by Ben Elton.

In the summer of 1981, Coyote appeared in *Fundamental Frolics*, a concert in aid of Mencap, which was filmed and shown on BBC Two on the 31st July. The album of the concert, which was on 1st June, was released in November.

Rik appeared in a number of movies during 1981

too, including *Eye Of The Needle*, *An American Werewolf In London*, *Couples And Robbers*, *Shock Treatment*, and *The Orchard End Murder*. He also had a role, alongside Alexei Sayle and Keith Allen, in the ITV drama *Wolcott*.

Around this time producers at Granada Television were in early development of a show designed to be a spiritual successor to *Not The Nine O'Clock News*. Sandy Ross had recently been producing the Saturday morning show *Mersey Pirate*, but this summer he was at the Edinburgh Fringe.

> *'"The idea for a late night comedy revue programme has been here at Granada for four or five years," he says. Granada spent three months' viewing productions at the Edinburgh Festival and elsewhere last year to select a suitable cast for the programmes.'*
>
> (THE STAGE, 8TH JULY 1982)

It must have been a lengthy search, but it was the Perrier winning Footlights revue that landed the gig, alongside an emerging face from the alternative world.

> *'Sandy Ross ... approached the talented stand-up comic Rik Mayall in 1982 to write and star in a three-show series initially called There's Nothing To Worry About! Mayall agreed and persuaded the TV company to sign up Ben Elton as well as some other artists to work on the show. Granada agreed but*

then, out of the blue, Mayall left to pursue something else, leaving Granada with Elton, Fry, Laurie, Thompson, Redmond and Paul Shearer.'

(HUGH LAURIE: THE BIOGRAPHY, ANTHONY BUNKO, PG)

There's Nothing To Worry About! aired in June of 1982 in the Granada region, before later being picked up by the wider network for a longer run, and renamed *Alfresco*.

Beginning in September of 1981, *The Comic Strip* left London and began a national tour that took in places like Sheffield Polytechnic (29th September) and Reading University (5th December).

'Comic Strip Is Here For Laughs - Reading concertgoers get the chance to sample some of London's outrageous alternative comedy this weekend. The Comic Strip is appearing at the University Students' Union on Saturday night after a successful season in London and some 25 dates in the provinces.'

(READING EVENING POST, 4TH DECEMBER 1981)

Throughout 1981 strikes had raged, bombs had exploded, the Labour party split, Murdoch bought *The Times*, 23 mines were closed, public spending was cut further, unemployment hit more than 10% of the workforce (2.68 million), Brixton rioted (as well as dozens of other towns and cities), Ken Livingstone became the leader of the GLC, 200,00 marched for jobs, and Thatcher's approval ratings reached an all-time low.

That autumn also saw the arrival of *A Kick Up The Eighties*, a sketch show produced by Colin Gilbert for BBC Two, and starring Tracey Ullman, Richard Stilgoe, Miriam Margolyes, Roger Sloman, Ron Bain, and one Rik Mayall.

> *'Someone had asked me to an audition ... I didn't realise that you were supposed to have prepared something to perform so they could see if you were any good ... on the spot I invented a character ... his name was Kevin Turvey.'*
>
> (THE RIK MAYALL, PG 51)

A more contemporaneous account of this appeared in an article in the *Reading Evening Post*, in March of 1984.

> *'Some years ago he was asked to film a pilot show for Granada Television with fellow comedian Alexei Sayle ... he was uncertain about when filming was to take place and when he phoned Alexei, was horrified to learn it was the following day. "I didn't know what to do and as we were sitting on the train the next day I had a blank notebook while Alexei had reams of brilliant material. So in the end, I went in to the studio, put on a Brummie accent and talked about nothing."'*
>
> (READING EVENING POST, 31ST MARCH 1984)

(The picture this paints is remarkably similar to the scene on the train in *The Young Ones* as they head for *University Challenge*.)

I think the article's author is conflating an audition with a studio recording, and Rik himself seems to be mistaking the early pre-production work on *There's Nothing To Worry About* with BBC Scotland's casting for theirs. But it's interesting that the producers were considering Alexei Sayle for the show too. In a later re-telling of the story, Rik correctly remembers it was a screen test for Sean Hardie and Tom Gutteridge, the former of whom suggested the *Investigates* format, while the latter went out and bought the blue anorak from C&A. (Oxford Student Magazine, 2001)

Mayall was not billed under his own name on *A Kick Up The Eighties*, instead being credited as Kevin Turvey. In an interview with Jeremy Pascall for *Company Magazine* (June,1982), Rik thinks it's a shame that Kevin was on a comedy show, thinking it may have been better for him to be on *Newsnight*.

> *'I originally intended him to appear as a real reporter giving a round-up of the week's events. That would have been very exciting; people not knowing whether he's real – this bloke rambling completely off the point, totally screwing it up.'*

Turvey (not Rik) even appeared on an edition of *Russell Harty* on the 3rd November 1981.

'He subjected a noticeably nervous Harty to one of Turvey's exquisitely banal ramblings, replete with gawping eyes, twisted hand gestures and a visual nightmare of suburban bad taste clothing. Later in the programme Mayall reappeared in the middle of Harty's chat with Costello to let him know that if he was driving a bus through the desert and came across a stranded Harty, he'd — wait for it! — take him to the wrong bus station!'

(TALKING TURVEY WITH RIK MAYALL, STEVE TAYLOR, THE FACE, JANUARY 1982)

It's wrong to characterise Harty as nervous, he was playing along brilliantly, and it's well worth a watch if you can find the clip.

Mayall saw out the year writing on a Hogmanay special for BBC Scotland. *81 Take 2* was produced by Sean Hardie, and was broadcast at 11.20pm. The show featured *The Hee Bee Gee Bees*, Robbie Coltrane, and Celia Imrie.

All this is to say that up until this point, Rik and Ade had barely appeared on TV screens together. Something Rik was asked about by Steve Taylor in *The Face*.

'I feel really good working with him: having been together for five years we're very mutually supportive. If I shit out he can cover me with an ad-libbed line ... We sat down and had a long talk about careers a couple of years ago when we did a student drama

festival in Durham and got a slagging from The Guardian. We had a long chat about our responsibility to each other and decided that we should work together because we do work well together. But, we'd never hold each other back ... Ade's strength is small, subtle, theatre stuff, films and absurdist acting. He's very photogenic. He's got a part in The Young Ones, a sitcom I'm involved in preparing for ITV, and he's got a film part coming up. Coyote will continue.'

Wait, what? *The Young Ones* was being developed by ITV? I can find no other reference to this at the moment, so I'm going to assume that's an error, and should say the BBC.

That film part of Ade's was as Larry in *The Magnificent One.*

1982

This was a year that began as the coldest ever on record, with temperatures dropping to -27C in Aberdeenshire. Meanwhile, unemployment would break the three million mark, just as Mark Thatcher was getting lost in the Sahara, and his mother's approval ratings would sky-rocket as a result of the Falklands War.

Mitch, as played by Rik, formed a chunk of *Wood And Walters* which was on ITV at roughly the same time that the pilot for *The Young Ones* was being shot (end of January 1982).

> *'[Mitch] isn't supposed to be very funny. I wasn't looking for a laugh but for people to react with 'yeuch' … Just as I wanted Kevin to appear on a serious show, I wanted Mitch to do something serious on a comedy show … [he] was a bit of agitprop but I don't feel I have to make people recognise truth.'*

(LET'S HEAR IT FOR RIK MAYALL, COMPANY, JUNE 1982)

Rik had a brush with the TV version of *Whoops Apocalypse* before his wider role in the movie. He appears in the second episode, which aired on the 21st March 1982. And a couple of months later, he starred alongside Judy Parfitt and Annette Crosby in *Northern Lights*, an STV television movie that aired on LWT in May. He claims he misread the script and said Yes by accident (The Face).

Throughout the first half of 1982, the *Comic Strip* continued touring the UK, playing at the Oxford Apollo in February, before heading to Australia for two months to appear at the Adelaide Festival and in Sidney and Melbourne (Last Laugh Theatre Restaurant, 22nd March – 3rd April), and elsewhere. Michael White, writing in the student magazine *Tharunka*, said 'It's rather difficult to make a critical judgement of a cabaret show which is forced into the wide open spaces of a theatre. The cushy comfort and the microwave quiches do not sit easily on the stomach of an audience which has come to catch some of the abundant drool which flows from the punk-envenomed poster lips of the *Comic Strip's* Rick Mayall.' (Tharunka, 13th April 1982)

Much of the first series of *The Young Ones* was written by Rik and Lise Mayer in Australia during this tour.

The summer months saw few live appearances from Rik or Ade (though Rik did appear as Kevin and others at the Glastonbury CND Festival in June), mostly because they were filming *The Comic Strip* and in the studio (and on location in Bristol) recording *The Young Ones.*

> *'Only days after axing one controversial TV show the BBC is about to launch another. Bernard Falk's Sin On Saturday was killed off because "it did not reach satisfactory standards." Now four outrageous young men are to walk the TV tightrope between instant fame and failure. Their humour makes the Not the Nine O'Clock News team look like Sunday school teachers. The only innocent thing about the series is the title: The Young Ones. Their language is vulgar and their brand of comedy shocking.'*

> (DAILY MIRROR, 28TH AUGUST 1982)

So, the next we saw the duo on our screens was on Monday 13th September at 9pm on BBC Two.

Kevin Turvey: The Man Behind The Green Door was the show Rik promised in his interview in The

Face.

> *'Kevin's quite a hot property in the business sense. [I] could sell the idea, do videos and all that, but I'm not interested. In fact I'm going to knock Kevin on the head, once I've done a half-hour documentary about him.'*

The Man Behind The Green Door featured Ade Edmondson as Keith Marshall, while Raw Sex became members of Kevin's band, appropriately called *20th Century Coyote*.

> *'I've never seen anybody take the piss out of documentaries yet. The ones I've seen have been very well presented and quite interesting. To see one that's completely off the point, that doesn't know where it's going, that is appallingly filmed and edited should be very funny.'*

(COMPANY)

Through part of the year, viewers could see Rik briefly, dressed as an astronaut, trying to eat a chocolate bar, in an advert for the now defunct *5-4-3-2-1*. He also narrated some sketches (which he also wrote) about the adventures of Dave The Cardbox Box in the first series of *Carrott's Lib* (broadcast from 2nd October onwards).

And then, on the 2nd November, on the launch night of Channel 4, *The Comic Strip* presented *Five Go Mad In Dorset*, which was watched by 3.35

million people. It starred Adrian Edmondson as Dick, with nary a peep from Rik.

It's amazing to think that up until this point, Rik and Ade aren't really a fixed double act in the viewers' minds.

Or maybe you were lucky enough to be in the studio audience back in January, watching *Demolition* being taped. Or even there from the end of July through to the start of September, watching them shoot *Flood, Interesting, Boring, Oil,* and *Bomb,* in that order.

Either way, when *The Young Ones* hit BBC Two screens on Tuesday 9th November at 9pm, it's fair to say that Rick and Vyvyan planted Rik and Ade indelibly into the TV audiences' mind as a double act, even if there was little written reaction from the critics. But that was by design.

> *'The way Kevin sort of slipped into people's lives was good. We wanted the same with the Young Ones, we didn't want critics telling people it was good. Then it wouldn't have belonged to them or to us. It's a great feeling if you allow people to discover something for themselves...'*

(ROGUE MAYALL, DAVE MCCULLOUGH, SOUNDS, 11TH DECEMBER 1982)

The series highest rated episode was Interesting, on the 7th December, watched by 3.55 million, making it the channel's sixth most watched show, tying with, interestingly, *Russell Harty*. When the first series was repeated the following May, it did even better, with *Bomb*, on 19th May, watched by 3.9 million.

Rik got his wish. The show arrived with very little fanfare, and the audience was left to find the show for itself. Ken Irwin did mention it though, on the day of the first episode, in the *Daily Mirror*.

> *'A new comedy team hits the screen tonight. But be warned … this will be no innocent comedy romp. It involves four outrageous characters living together as squatters in a derelict house. They're a pretty shocking mob and their behaviour — and their language— is likely to upset older viewers …'*

Later in the article, producer Paul Jackson says:

> *'We were taking a big chance. When the first script was submitted, no one was quite sure if it would work. But I think it's the most exciting new comedy we've done in years.'*

In a different piece a few years later, Jackson revealed how he persuaded BBC bosses to commission the show in the first place.

> *'In order to convince the then head of light entertainment Jimmy Gilbert, Jackson sat down with the three writers one Sunday afternoon and recorded it on an audio cassette which was then performed to the powers that be. "Hearing it performed*

Rik goes on to add 'we had to cut certain words from sketches because they were considered too naughty by the BBC. We are not trying to push censorship back. But when you use swear words in normal life, and then you're not allowed to use them on TV, it's difficult to understand.' (Daily Mirror, 9th November 1982)

There aren't that many contemporary TV reviews to find about the show either. There's one by Ron Knox, which in part reads:

> *'Auntie Beeb looks like having another 'Monty Python'-type cult success on their hands with 'The Young Ones' … When you reflect on what has happened at the end of each episode, it is difficult to see how it appeared so funny at the time. The answer, or course, lies in the timing … and Rik Mayall, one of the most original comic talents to emerge for years … This exercise in collective lunacy will undoubtedly win over more and more converts, with the notable exception of lentil lovers.'*

A few weeks later, on 11th December, Hilary Kingsley reviewed the series in the *Daily Mirror*, calling it 'the most original comedy of the year' and suggesting that 'a second series would be smashing'.

But at this point, there was no talk of a second series. Indeed, Rik is quoted in the *Mirror* saying 'we don't know if we want to do another series like this next year, or if we should keep moving forwards and so something a bit more extreme.' (Daily Mirror, 7th December 1982)

With each repeat run in 1983, '84, and '85, more and more people found *The Young Ones*. The repeat of *Interesting* in 1985 was watched by 6.48 million viewers. It was only a matter of time before there was a second series.

1983

It appeared to rain blood in January, as red rain fell from the sky, caused by sand from the Sahara. Breakfast television began for the first time in the UK, with *Breakfast Time* competing with *TV-am*. The Tories cut taxes again, and thus spending, just before announcing a General Election. They went on to win a majority of 144 seats, a turnaround from their low polling of the previous years.

1983 was a relatively quiet year for both Rik and Ade in terms of television appearances. They did of course star in various editions of *The Comic Strip Presents ...* (of which, more later) but most of their time was spent touring a live show called *Kevin Turvey And The Bastard Squad Featuring The Young Ones* – something Rik mentions in *Sound* magazine:

> *'I'm writing for these live dates at the present. Then there's a radio show coming up, Kevin's Top Fifty! and also two books.'*

Rehearsals for the tour were held at the Irish Club on Eaton Square, in Belgravia, with a musical trio set to join Rik, Ade, and Nigel Planer on stage in a similar vein to the earlier *Comic Strip* tour. Amanda Simmons completed the retinue, performing a version of *These Boots Are Made For Walking* that Roland Rivron says Rik greeted off stage with howls of appreciation (What The F*** Did I Do Last Night, Roland Rivron pg 101-103).

Lise Mayer also travelled on the tour, so that she and Rik could start writing the next series of *The Young Ones* (Rivron believes), and helping to re-write and hone the live show.

> *'Kevin Turvey is appearing at Reading University on Tuesday night – but all tickets have been sold so you'll have to catch him at the Slough Fulcrum on March 17 instead.'*

(READING EVENING POST, 5TH MARCH 1983)

> *'The sell-out visit of Midlands pop humorist Kevin Turvey to Derby Assembly Rooms has been postponed for a week – "due to unforeseen circumstances" says Derby City entertainments manager Mr Alf Fullerton. All 1,600 tickets for the March 24 visit have*

been sold for some weeks. The tickets are now valid for the new date Thursday 31 March.'

(DERBY DAILY TELEGRAPH, 9TH MARCH 1983)

Likewise, the Ipswich Gaumont date was moved from 25th March to the 4th April (Haverhill Echo, 17th March 1983).

'Like Topsy, Turvey just growed on this packed audience at Derby Assembly Rooms last night. He insulted them, hurled obscenities at them and his fans, mainly teenagers-plus, howled for more.

'Rik Mayall – now the open secret of the real(?) name of Kevin Turvey – brought along his friends Neil and Adrian (who could also be Keith and Vyv) and the singing girl in a black dress. And no matter how bad or good they were, they couldn't do a thing wrong.

'Having called off the original date last week, they last night kept the audience waiting more than 45 minutes and then burst in to a reception that must have had the Assembly Rooms management reaching for the return booking contracts.

'Kevin and his mates are a new breed of stand-up comics with a line of humour that is lavatorial at best, graffiti-like in general

and over the top into the obscene without the least incitement.

'It is easy to say that the trio's material is puerile and their talent non-existent but their timing is almost instinctive, their characters original gems of acting and the way they put it all together indicates a very real talent and a precise rapport with their audience.

'Rik, Kevin, or whatever is naturally a very funny man. And if you don't like his style you can do what it says on the wall – and what he doesn't hesitate to tell you to do.'

(GD HAMMERTON, DERBY DAILY TELEGRAPH, 1ST APRIL 1983)

The tour culminated in an appearance at the Apollo Victoria Theatre in London, as part of the Sizewell B protest concert *Too Hot To Handle*. Rik, Adrian, and Nigel performed as their Young Ones characters, singing a version of *My Generation*.
The tour was chronicled in an article by Joe Hosken for *Soundmaker* magazine, and Roland Rivron writes about it in his excellent book *What The F*** Did I Do Last Night?*. It began badly, when the troupe arrived in Sheffield:

'As we pulled into Sheffield around lunchtime, the first thing we noticed was the abundance of posters advertising

*forthcoming attractions, from Def Leppard
to Victoria Wood. Try as we might, no-one
could spot a poster for 'Straight From TV! –
The Young Ones! – Live On Stage!'.*

*'"Not to worry,' someone said. "This happens
if the show gets sold out enough in advance,
so there is no need to waste money putting
posters up."*

*'... there had been some sort of cock-up, and
we were exactly a month early ...*

*'And so it was that Rik, Ade and Nigel
were despatched to local radio stations to let
everyone know that The Young Ones were in
town and playing that night. Not the best of
starts to a nationwide tour, but it kept us on
our toes.'*

(WHAT THE F*** DID I DO LAST NIGHT, PG 103-4)

They played to a packed house for four and half
hours.

The Nottingham date didn't get started until gone
11pm, but still ran for two and half hours, even
if the tour band The Ken Bishop Nice Twelve,
featuring Simon Brint and Damien Pew, as well as
Rivron, protested that their adrenaline levels were
shot.

As the tour went on, things got tighter and
more developed. Early shows featured Mortimer

Vaughn, a character played by Nigel Planer, which never quite worked and was dropped. It sounds to me, at least, that Vaughn was a prototype for Ralph Filthy, so it wasn't all for nothing. Nigel confirmed this thought to me in a tweet when I asked him about it.

Ade also developed his Adrian Bastard character on the road, as well as reviving Keith Marshall from *Behind The Green Door*. And together, as Vyv and Neil, they sang a duet called *Lentil Nightmare*.

At the end of the tour, Rik and Ade began writing *Dirty Movie* for the second series of *The Comic Strip Presents ...*

The first series had only just aired a few months before, in January, with a repeat of *Five Go Mad In Dorset*, and debuts for *War*, *The Beat Generation*, *Bad News Tour*, and *Summer School* – strange for a British series to only have five episodes.

Bad News was broadcast a good fourteen months before *This Is Spinal Tap* ever arrived in cinemas, and was written by Adrian Edmondson. It featured Rik and Nigel as his band mates, and followed a documentary style, much like *Behind The Green Door*, and was inspired by Mark Kidal's 1976 BBC documentary *So You Wanna Be A Rock 'n' Roll Star?*. They filmed it in the autumn of 1982.

So, why did this first series run only have five episodes, rather than the standard six? Contemporaneous accounts suggest that there was to be a sixth film called *Back To Normal with Eddie Monsoon*, written by Adrian Edmondson. As late as 17th January 1983, the *Daily Mirror* ran a full page spread about Peter Richardson entitled *Horribly Funny*.

> *'Future treats include some pretty dreadful times on the road with a heavy metal band in Bad News Tour and the chat show to end them all – the Eddie Monsoon show.'*

And yet it was never broadcast.

On the day of the final episode, *Summer School*, Tony Pratt reported in the *Mirror*:

> *'Channel 4 chat show gets chop. The shock-horror tactics of Britain's liveliest new television team, The Comic Strip, have begun to worry even their broad-minded bosses at Channel 4. The team decided to drop an episode from their current series which ends tonight ... The group had planned a show called The Eddie Monsoon Chat Show. But Channel 4 executives frowned when they saw the script ... Dawn French said: "It wasn't dirty but it was very abrasive. We didn't want to change it, so rather than argue at this stage we decided to hold it over and try again for next series."'*

(DAILY MIRROR, 31ST JANUARY 1983)

This certainly suggests that discussions were ongoing right up to broadcast. The script for the episode appears in the script book published by

Methuen.

Something else filmed in 1982 but released widely in 1983 was *Dead On Time*, a short film starring Rowan Atkinson that appeared in cinemas from 4th February onwards, and features a hoard of comedy greats, including a small cameo from Adrian Edmondson.

Just before the *Bastard* tour, Rik appeared at *An Evening For Nicaragua*, a benefit concert organised by Andy De La Tour for the Nicaragua Solidarity Campaign. Andy hosted the event at the Shaftesbury Theatre, and introduced Kevin Turvey as well as Alexei Sayle and Julie Christie.

> *'The evening's entertainment will consist of a mixture of music and comedy, punctuated by readings on Nicaragua and its history. There will also be a raffle.'*

> (MARYLEBONE MERCURY, 11TH FEBRUARY 1983)

The benefit was filmed, and appeared later in the year on Channel 4 on 1st September. Turvey's appearance can often be found on YouTube.

In May, Adrian Edmondson appeared at the Lyric Theatre in Hammersmith in a play called *The White Glove*.

> *'Richard Maher and Roger Michell ... have returned with another literary jest. Moving from Chandler to Chekhov, they speculate on what happened after the end of 'The Cherry Orchard', after Madame Ranievskaia and her*

troupe have left the house with the sound of the woodman's axe ringing in their ears.'

(THE STAGE, 5TH MAY 1983)

'Adrian Edmondson, of the punk comedy TV series The Comic Strip and The Young Ones, plays the classic roles of Trofimov and Gayev, while Anthony Kiggings and Ian McNeice break into the deserted house as a couple of detectives who just might be Sherlock Holmes and Dr Watson. Chekhov will never be the same again!'

(READING EVENING POST, 23RD APRIL 1983)

Come August, and the Edinburgh Fringe festival was still a rather small affair, compared to these days. Andy De La Tour and Ben Elton were preparing to take their joint show up for a few weeks.

'Rik Mayall wasn't supposed to be on the bill. Ben Elton and I had planned to come to the Edinburgh Festival to do some stand-up comedy and with luck entice a hundred or so punters a night to come to see us. Ben wasn't yet well known as a performer, even though ... The Young Ones, had become a cult smash ... However, when we told our pal Rik we were coming to Edinburgh, he just said: "How could you two bastards go to the Festival without me?" ... We got ourselves

booked into the 300-seat venue in the Assembly Rooms and packed out the entire … festival, most seats sold even before we arrived. One evening Billy Connolly turned up to see the show and we had to squeeze him into the lighting box.'

(ANDY DE LA TOUR: RIK MAYALL AND ANARCHIC DAYS AT THE FRINGE, THE SUNDAY TIMES, 14TH AUGUST 2014)

The tickets list the show as *Standup Comedy: Ben Elton, Andy De La Tour and 20th Century Coyote*, but some of the listings around the time name Rik Mayall specifically. This is because the original plan had been to feature Rik and Ade, but according to the *A History Of Comedy In Several Objects* podcast (episode 35), no-one quite remembers why Ade didn't go up (but it was likely due to his commitments to *The White Glove*). Rik explained this discrepancy with the name on the tickets, claiming Ade had been hit by a bus, tearing up on stage, then revealing he was joking and they all fell for it (Character Assassination, Blitz magazine, November 1983).

Archive material from the time show that it was as late as mid-May when the plan changed. Back in February, Andy and Ben had even asked Jenny Lecoat to join them. She agreed, but later graciously stood aside to allow Rik and/or Ade to go up instead, a decision she later admitted was a great one, because she was no way near ready for the Assembly Rooms (episode 35).

The three of them took Standup Comedy out again,

this time in November and December, appearing Leicester University (20th Nov), the Alhambra in Bradford (27th Nov), and the Liverpool Playhouse (11th December).

On the 9th December, the *Liverpool Echo* announced that 'by popular demand ... this Sunday an extra performance has been added to a show called Standup Comedy featuring three modern-day parodists – Rik Mayall, Andy De La Tour and Ben Elton ... "We didn't realise they were so popular, but we're delighted that they agreed to put on an extra show".'

The next day, the same paper featured an interview with Rik by Peter Trollope. It features a remarkable quote from Rik:

> *'I want to do more theatre next year. There is an offer of a film, possibly about The Young Ones, but that's still only an idea at the moment.'*

(LIVERPOOL ECHO, 10TH DECEMBER 1983)

A review, also in the *Echo*, on 12th December, gives an insight into the make up of the show.

> *'With a back-drop of glittery Christmas grotto ribbons described as 'shredded Bacofoil' by opener Ben Elton, we were led into a packed 90 minutes of fast-paced, irreverent observations of life in the eighties.'*

De La Tour was on next, doing half an hour, then

Rik closed, beginning with Kevin and ending with Rick. The reviewer Peter Grant describes Elton as venomous, hails De La Tour as the next Rowan Atkinson, and Mayall as self-assured but capable of far better.

This double performance in Liverpool came slap-bang in the middle of the run of *Man Equals Man*, a play by Brecht that Rik was appearing in over in Manchester at the Contact. It was directed by Richard Williams, and also starred Paul Bradley and Liz Brailsford. Rik mentions it in the interview with Trollope:

> *'The discipline is different. I'd forgotten how different working on a play can be.'*

A review, again in the *Echo*, calls it 'an uncomfortable mixture of zanyism, message-making and black comedy. It makes an odd choice for a Christmas show." (Liverpool Echo, 9th December 1983)

We can't leave 1983 behind without talking about Mad Gerald.

Rik appeared (uncredited) in *The Black Seal*, the final episode of *The Black Adder* on Wednesday 20th July. In his marvellously exhaustive *The True History Of The Black Adder*, JF Roberts reveals that 'from the moment Rik showed up on set, he was in charge of the creation of Mad Gerald.' He goes on to quote John Lloyd, the show's producer, who says that Rik re-wrote his entire part.

Rik was in Glasgow for two studio recordings in August, performing some investigations for the second series of *A Kick Up The Eighties*. And some time this year, Natwest began an ad campaign to attract young savers, using a Vyvyan-like character, played by Edmondson, who smartens himself up to get a new account. This is the advert that the Postman refers to backstage in the *Nasty* episode of *The Young Ones*.

I always find it just as fascinating to learn what wasn't made. As the year died slowly in the swills of booze, bongs, and bad decisions at midnight, and 1984 waited patiently in the wings, Rik gave an interview to *The Times Educational Supplement*. In it, he mentions something he turned down.

> *'Recently he was asked to appear in television publicity for the Youth Training Scheme. He turned it down. "They gave me an outline but wanted me to do my own dialogue. Anyway, from what I've read it's a complete rip off and I don't want anything to do with it…"'*

(TES, 30TH DEC 1983).

This is also one of the first times that he mentions the second series of *The Young Ones*.

Ade saw out the year with the first showing of *Five Go Mad On Mescalin*, the follow up to the opening instalment of *The Comic Strip Presents …* which aired on the 3rd November.

1984

Hurricane force winds battered Britain, and the Government continued to curtail the rights of the Trades Unions. The long Miner's Strike was soon to begin, with the Battle of Orgreave in June ahead. Unemployment now stood at 3.26 million, with more people out of work than during the Great Depression.

The second series of *A Kick Up The Eighties* marked the move into 1984, with a four episode run, again featuring Kevin Turvey. This would be Kevin's last investigations on TV, though he appeared on stage after this.

Just a few days later, on 7th January, *The Comic Strip* presented *Dirty Movie*, a brilliant stand alone with Rik and Ade, and also starring Nigel Planer and French and Saunders. Ade co-wrote it with Peter Richardson.

> *'My act with Ade was always a crossover between acting and comedy. We've just done one of the Comic Strip films for the new series called Dirty Movie which I'm very pleased with because it's just exactly what we used to do in the early days. It's got a real absurdist feel to it. It's the first one hopefully of a huge crop – it looks odd and it looks good. It's just about a bloke who gets a dirty movie through the post and happens to own a cinema, and he's got to get everyone out so that he can watch it. Perhaps it's not yet quite absurdist enough for my taste...'*

(CHARACTER ASSASSINATION, BLITZ, NOVEMBER 1983)

Ade appeared in the following episode *Susie*, and both Rik and Ade were in *A Fistful of Traveller's Cheques* the next week. This time Rik co-wrote it with Richardson and Pete Richens.

On Monday 23rd January, studio recordings began on the second series of *The Young Ones*. The two recording days that week were to shoot *Sick*.

> *'Mayall admits that mistakes were made in the first series … Mayall got a letter from a teacher who understood that the point of the [racist policeman] joke was rather heavy handed anti-police satire, but found that the one black boy in her class was having the same abuse levelled at him. "In the next series, we'll be more careful", says Mayall, ruefully.'*

(CULT OF THE SNARL, TES, 30TH DECEMBER 1983)

The rest of the series was filmed each week over the coming weeks, until a strike interrupted the production. As a result, *Time* and *Summer Holiday* were delayed until the end of April, when both shows were recorded in one week. (DirtyFeed website)

As an aside, I know exactly where I was when they were filming the exterior scenes for the bank raid in *Summer Holiday*. I was sitting in my Gran's breakfast room in her house, playing with my toy cars on the carpet. I know this because my brother and sister went out for a walk with my Granddad, and when they returned they were showing off their new fancy notebooks. On their walk down the Gloucester Road, they'd stumbled on a BBC OB Unit, a yellow enflamed Anglia, and a big red London bus. And in their notebooks, they had autographs from Rik, Ade, Nigel, and Christopher. I wish I knew where those books were now.

Whilst Rik and Ade were in and out of the BBC Studios, they also appeared in the *Comic Strip's Gino* together, and Ade finally made his debut as Eddie Monsoon, this time in *Eddie Monsoon – A Life?*.

In his interview for *Blitz*, Rik drops this interesting hint about a deleted or unfilmed scene from *A Life?*, as well as revealing the original title for the episode.

> *'Well over a year ago he said that he'd give Kevin Turvey the boot as he'd already outlived his purpose. But at the tail end of '83 Turvey is still perhaps his hottest property, and still a 15 minute opener for his 40 minute act. Mayall's just finished filming a new Comic Strip episode called Eddie Monsoon (and his Talking Penis) in which, he says, Turvey bows out for good.'*

During the break in studio time for *The Young Ones*, there was a one-off re-staging of *Standup Comedy*, with Rik, Ben and Andy, at the Hexagon in Reading on 1st April.

'In these days of sitcoms and high tech special effects it is good to see there is still room for human talent unadorned by trickery. Last night's show at the Hexagon presented three stand-up comedians who got the warmest reception I have seen in a long time from a traditionally sticky audience. Star of the show was Rik Mayall who divided his act between his alter ego Kevin Turvey and a string of gags told as himself. His Kevin, of TV's Kick Up The 80s fame, was delivered in a deadpan Brummie accent and relaying the details of his day in the kind of excruciatingly minute detail that is incredibly boring in real life but very funny on stage. He even managed to delay his entrance on stage, claiming he was running late and gave us a running commentary via the PA system of his journey from the station.'

(READING EVENING POST, 2ND APRIL 1984)

A repeat run of the first series of *The Comic Strip Presents ...* ran at the same time as this, and then, on Tuesday 8th May, at 9pm on BBC Two, *Bambi* ushered in the second series of *The Young Ones*. 4.35 million welcomed the Bachelor Boys back to their screens, and the series peaked with *Sick*, watched by 5.05 million, the second most watched show of the week on BBC Two. They even made the front cover of the *Radio Times*, albeit with a publicity shot from the first series.

On *Breakfast Time*, Lise Mayer revealed that this provoked letters of complaint saying 'we don't want pictures of these kinds of people in our homes.'

Rik spoke to *NME* about their approach to writing the second series.

> *'We've tried to make it exciting and unpredictable but obviously you haven't got the joy of seeing those characters for the first time, like you had with the first series. It was actually funny to just see Vyvyan, but now you've got to concentrate on him doing something funny rather than just being there. We tried to make the quality of the writing better. Everyone was much more confident as writers and performers... and we knew there was a huge expectation this time.*

> *'Last time it was alright as no one knew what to expect... and the longer it goes back the more brilliant people think it is. So if anything we tried to change it by making sure there were many more gags, making sure the gags were better written and better shot. And if anything we tried to make it nastier, make them less cute.'*

(RIK WITH A SILENT P, NME, 4TH AUGUST 1984)

Adrian voiced Harold Angryperson in the seventh episode of the first series of *Spitting Image* on the 13th May. He also provided the voice for characters in an advert for Lego Castle that aired around this time, even doing a fairly good impression of Kevin Turvey. And he appeared in the flesh as he made a music video with Tracey Ullman for her single *Sunglasses*. The shoot for this made the gossip page in the *Daily Mirror*.

> *'Tracey had a frightening time making the video. She says: "During one scene the two of us were rowing out to sea when we lost both oars. It frightened the life out of me but Adrian seemed to enjoy it all. Luckily, we were rescued a few minutes later by another boat."'*

(DAILY MIRROR, 21ST JULY 1984)

Rik appeared in a music video himself, playing a kind of Bond villain in Lionheart's *Die For Love*. The band defeat him with a weird mix of karate, guns, and guitars.

Through the summer of 1984, the Miner's Strike continued, unemployment hit an all time high, and the government changed the law to require a ballot for strikes (I hope you're satisfied Thatcher). So a *Gala Evening For The Miners* was held on the 7th September at the Royal Festival Hall. Rik performed alongside Alexei Sayle, Nigel Planer, Wham!, and The Style Council.

And then, one weekend at the end of September, something so odd and remarkable occurred that unless a film crew (produced by LWT and Paul Jackson) had been there to capture it all, no one would quite believe it happened. Stars of music and screen descended, for no fee, on the Hampshire village of Nether Wallop for their inaugural International Arts Festival. It was organised by Jane Tewson as a response to Edinburgh after she read an article by Stephen Pile in *The Times* asking why the village couldn't do one of its own.

Rik sang on stage with Jools Holland and Bill Wyman, Peter Cook and Mel Smith did a sketch together, Billy Connolly and Rowan Atkinson performed, as did Fry And Laurie.

The festival raised money for the village, and Jane Tewson says that it provided the spark for the foundation of *Comic Relief* a year later, which she co-founded with Richard Curtis. The whole, unbelievable affair was turned into the documentary *Weekend In Wallop*, which aired on ITV on 30th December.

Just a few days later, and Rik barges into a sketch on *The Lenny Henry Show*, playing a frustrated comedy writer demanding to know why his material isn't being used. While Lenny Henry seems a natural fit for Rik (and Ade, who pops up in a separate episode), the same can't be said for *Canon And Ball*, whose show Rik appeared on in November, running circles around them, and even seeming to visibly irritate Bobby Ball as he steals the scene.

On the 27th October, Rik made a rare appearance as himself on an episode of *Wogan*. After performing as Rick (which Terry clearly enjoyed), he sat down with the host and had a self-effacing chat. It's remarkable to see the physical transformation from the unattractive character in to the devilishly handsome man. They discussed the demise of *The Young Ones*, and Rik suggested that the book *Bachelor Boys* was the third series, because it contains all new material. When Terry asked what the aim of the show had been:

> *"Just make it as exciting as the Pythons were. I remember watching them and being so disappointed when half an hour was over, because they really used the television set really well, anything could happen, and that's what we tried to do with The Young Ones. We tried to get three strands of sitcom, variety, and revue shows, and bang them all in together so that you didn't know what to expect."*

This appearance was to plug the new book *Bachelor Boys*, by Elton, Mayer, and Mayall, and was mentioned in the 8th November edition of the *Daily Mirror*.

> *'A week ago he appeared on, of all things, the WOGAN show!!! With Raquel*

Welch, who's nearly old enough to be his Grannie!!! He's just helped write a Young Ones book, which is a BEST-SELLER already. He turned up the other morning with co-authors Ben Elton and Lise Mayer on boring old BREAKFAST TELEVISION with old uncle FRANK BOUGH!!! And [he] fitted in a weekend CANON and BALL TV show. Soon he sets off on a comedy tour and is preparing to appear in Gogol's The Government Inspector.'

(DAILY MIRROR, 8TH NOVEMBER 1984)

The tour was another one with Ben Elton, and had begun in the middle of October. It ended in December, by way of more than twenty venues, including the Southport Theatre, where Tony Darrow saw them.

'Any act which can fill a fairly large seaside venue to capacity in the middle of winter deserves special recognition within show business circles. In December Rik Mayall and Ben Elton achieved the "House Full" feat not only at Southport Theatre but at an impressive string of other venues up and down the country ... Where such controversial "alternative comedy" material is concerned, there is bound to be dispute within the profession and among the public over the bounds of contemporary acceptability. Messrs Mayall and Elton rely

heavily upon lavatory and sex humour intentionally put over in the worst possible taste ... and undeleted expletives are offered instead of traditional punchlines. But the clear, hard fact is that this type of act is extraordinarily popular with younger audiences who are prepared to pay today's ticket prices. A show such as this is unusually inexpensive to mount, requiring the minimum in the way of sound and lighting effects and dispensing entirely with the need for musical accompaniment ... Ben Elton, worked his frantic way through a first half which earned him huge waves of unexpected laughter and applause. It requires the same sort of mental outlook to enjoy either of these left wing talents ... Here were fifty minutes of abusive humour delivered at break-neck speed, stand-up comedy on the run. Mayall played his first five minutes from the wings, heard but unseen as he described his journey to the theatre. When his famous Kevin Turvey character eventually arrived at the microphone a pre-heated crowd, cult fans of "The Young Ones", proved easy to please. Foul language dominated the next sixty minutes ... Later the same night, Mayall and Elton were entertaining a university crowd. Clearly their following among the student population is loyal and destined to be long term ... this type of act will never be given television time in the near future, a factor which will prolong the theatrical value of the alternative comedian.'

(THE STAGE, 20TH DECEMBER 1984)

The day after the tour ended, Rik was seen at the Palladium as part of *Stars On Sunday*.

1985

With half of all miners now on strike, things got rather dangerous in the new year, as Sir Adrian and Sir Richard made their debut on the pilot episode of *Saturday Live* (12th January). In their *Towering Inferno* sketch, Rik sets fire to Ade's trousers. In safety rehearsals, this had been done with him lying on the floor, but for the sketch he was standing upright on a chair. The flames rose faster than expected, and in the panic Adrian forgot his safety word. He suffered some burns to the legs, and singed eyebrows, but luckily the fire was put out before any more harm came of him.

1985 was otherwise a relatively quiet year for the pair on our TV screens, at least for new content, but both series of *The Young Ones* enjoyed a successful repeat run on BBC Two.

This was probably due to Rik appearing on stage in over 80 performances of *The Government Inspector* at the Olivier, running from January through to October. Written by Nikolai Gogol, the play is a comedy of errors that explores human greed and political corruption in Imperial Russia.

'Rik Mayall is the penurious clerk, at first afraid of being arrested, then preening in his unexpected glory. He gives a performance of rollicking energy blended with sensitive appreciation of his situation, both privately and publicly, and has at times a rippling sense of wit.'

(THE STAGE, 7TH FEBRUARY 1985)

Rik took a week or two off from the play in April to begin his 1985 tour with Ben Elton, arriving in Poole (21st), Southampton (22nd), Leicester (23rd), Oxford (24th), Nottingham (25th), Sunderland (26th), Hull (27th), Lincoln (28th), Hanley (29th), and Blackburn (30th). In to May, they took in Buxton (4th), Great Yarmouth (5th), Tunbridge Wells (6th), Barnstaple (7th), and ended at the Bristol Hippodrome (8th). This may have been timed to coincide with the repeat run of *The Young Ones*.

The Nottingham date at the Royal Concert Hall garnered two separate reviews. The first, the day after, read:

'Elton started with 40-minutes of hard-hitting moaning. No subject or person escaped his tongue as he dished out his "dangerous night of comedy". Drunks, real ale drinkers and students were hit first. He remembered the student bar with "the specially slowed down Space

Invader machines for medical students."
Advertising, jogging, designer labels and
double-entendres were also victims of his
satirical and rapid delivery, slightly too
ribald for print ... Mayall adopted a different
tack, though equally littered with the now
expected swearing ... The two hours passed
rapidly, both men using the stage and
audience to their advantage.'

(NOTTINGHAM EVENING POST, 26TH APRIL 1985)

Then a week later, in the *Mansfield And Sutton Recorder*:

'[Rik's] encore stunt of a small explosion in
a very private place must keep him sweating
night after night in case it goes wrong!'

(2ND MAY 1985)

Luckily, it didn't go wrong, because in June Rik rocked up to Television Centre, donned a blonde wig adorned with seashells, and literally blew the doors off of the *Blackadder* set as Lord Flashheart. It was a conscious effort to get away from his Rick persona, and was such an energised performance it left an indelible mark on the series. But it wouldn't be on TV until the next January.

At the beginning of August, the *Daily Mirror* announced Rik's *Late Late Show*.

'Young One Rik Mayall faces a daunting
challenge when he flies out to Ibiza next

week. Rik and his partner Ben Elton will be doing five shows for hundreds of very happy holidaymakers at the unearthly hour of 1.30 am. And Ben ... admits "It certainly is a challenge. By that time of the morning they will all be well oiled on Spanish plonk. We reckon if we can keep that lot happy, we can entertain anybody!"'

(DAILY MIRROR, 2ND AUGUST 1985)

When they got back, they played a date at the Cornwall Coliseum. That was just a couple of days after Jimmy Tarbuck played there. On a whim, I went back to look if they shared some other venues at such similar times, and sure enough, Tarby played the Royal Concert Hall in Nottingham too. A part of me hopes that this served as some sort of genesis for *Filthy, Rich And Catflap* - as Ben and Rik arrived at a venue to hear all the showbiz tales from the staff about Jimmy's visit, and between them created the prototype for Richie Rich.

'Jimmy Tarbuck never seems comfortable as a television game show host. But last night on stage ... he settled into a firecracker routine of jokes and songs ... Yes, we'd heard a lot of them before.'

(NOTTINGHAM EVENING POST, 23RD APRIL 1985)

At the start of October, the long run of *The Government Inspector* came to an end, and on the 11th, Rik turned up on *The Tube*, pretending to be drunk – perhaps in response to his first appearance.

> *'Last time Rik appeared on The Tube he got into trouble with TV bosses for using a four-letter word and upsetting viewers. He's been warned not to try it again.'*

(DAILY MIRROR, 11TH OCTOBER 1985)

Adrian in the meantime, had spent June and July in Derbyshire and Staffordshire, alongside Jennifer Saunders as they filmed *Happy Families*. Shot entirely on film, and written by Ben Elton, Paul Jackson had spent two years looking for someone to make it, and eventually landed it at BBC Manchester. Whilst announcing the production, Jackson also teased a second show to be made on the Oxford Road in the summer of **1986.** (The Stage, 30th May 1985)

Happy Families began on BBC One at 8.25pm on the 17th October. (During the same period, Saunders could be seen at half eight on ITV in the equally excellent sitcom *Girls On Top*, also produced by Jackson).

> *'The BBC's comedy event of the season is Happy Families. Cancel all Thursday night outings and don't argue! Ben Elton's script about the cantankerous grannie Fuddle, her four ghastly granddaughters, cretinous grandson, hideous housemaid and cook, is jam-packed with silliness and acted with*

(HILARY KINGSLEY, THE DAILY MIRROR, 19TH OCTOBER 1985)

Rik turns up in episode three as a Nazi priest.

On the 15th November, Adrian crashed through the wall of Wogan's set, and revealed his biggest comedy influence was Orville, is told the rudest word he's allowed to use is 'bum', and proceeds to drop two 'bollocks' instead – Terry has great fun along the way too. This all coincided with the release of the *Comic Strip's* first feature film *The Supergrass*. Back in April, Barry Norman aired an on location report from the shoot in which Ade admits he once French-kissed his Granny by mistake.

Rik and Ben saw the year out with their *Stand Up Tour 1985*, taking in a lot of venues in Scotland and the north before finishing with five nights at the Dominion Theatre in London.

Then we saw another one of those remarkable, incongruous mash ups of old wave and new, when the Dangerous Brothers celebrated Christmas with Noel Edmonds on his *Live Live Christmas Breakfast Show*. Noel seemed to thoroughly enjoy their brief company, as they promoted the upcoming inaugural *Comic Relief.*

1986

With the new year chimes still echoing in people's heads, Rik gave a marvellous present to The Kids on the 6th January 1986. Dressed as a more handsome version of Rick, he read *George's Marvellous Medicine* to young viewers on *Jackanory* over the course of the week.

The book was chosen by a viewer poll, as part of the show's 20th anniversary celebrations. I remember there being a furore about the dangers of kids emulating the antics and poisoning their parents, but looking at the papers of the time there's nary a mention of it. Rik did appear in the Broom Cupboard with Andy Crane though, during the repeat run in 1988, to warn viewers not to try any of it at home.

The year would see Michael Hesletine and Leon Brittan resign over the Westland Helicopters scandal, unemployment rise again to 14.4% of the workforce, the Wapping dispute, the abolition of the GLC, prison riots, and Labour nine-points ahead in MORI polls.

Also in January, after a prolonged absence, *The Comic Strip* were back on the small screen with new episodes. Rik and Ade appeared in *Consuela,* and *Private Enterprise*, which Adrian directed.

The Dangerous Brothers returned in January too, tearing their way through the entire first series of *Saturday Live*, and further establishing Rik and Ade as a double act in the minds of TV viewers.

January was jam packed, with Rik's episode of *Blackadder* (*Bells*) airing on the 9th. It was meant to be the second episode, but was instead chosen to open the new series, which was watched on BBC One by 10.65 million viewers.

Come February, Adrian began to spread his acting wings with a more serious role in Les Blair's *Screen Two* film *Honest, Decent And True*. He starred alongside Gary Oldman and Richard E Grant, in a satire about the advertising industry. This was the beginning of several collaborations with Blair, who came to Britain's attention as the director of *Law And Order*, a 1978 series that painted a controversial picture of the law and legal system.

Spring, and along came a Christmas miracle (well, March the 8th), as *The Young Ones* rose from the dead, and joined with Cliff Richard to sing about his disturbing *Living Doll*. Released as a fundraiser for the upcoming *Comic Relief*, the single reached number one in the UK, and the B side was *(All The Little Flowers Are) Happy*. And yes, the song's got a video, which was filmed in and around Chiswick.

(This wasn't the only music video Rik was in around March time either. He plays a loser type in *Butcher Bitches* by Circus Circus Circus.)

A clip from the *Living Doll* video was shown a few days later (12th) on *Wogan*, and Rik joined him on the chairs to talk about the *Comic Relief* project, looking devilishly handsome with his five o'clock shadow and cropped hair. He explains that they chose this song because it had some natural spaces in it for the comedy, and plugs the three live shows for the charity at the Shaftsbury Theatre (Rowan Atkinson's revue was on there at the time).

He also reveals that he's dressed in his costume for *Mr Jolly Lives Next Door*, which the *Comic Strip* team were filming that day.

Comic Relief went *Utterly Utterly Live* on the 4th, 5th, and 6th of April, and a compilation of those performances was broadcast on BBC One, as part of their *Omnibus* strand, on the 25th.

By then though, Rik and Ben were down in Australia, doing their *An Evening Of Stand Up* tour, which took in Melbourne, Sidney, Canberra, and Adelaide. The two stopped by the studio of *Sounds*, on the Seven Network, and gave an interview in which they revealed that together they were currently writing a new show in their hotel rooms that would be filmed in October and November. Rik also admits he had a problem with his trouser explosives in one of the shows, but doesn't go in to detail. The segment ends with the video for The Art Of Noise's *Peter Gunn* video, which stars Rik as a gumball American detective.

When they returned to the UK, Ben and Rik performed an *Evening of Standup Comedy* at the Cornwall Coliseum on 1st August.

Around this time too, Rik took time out to make a promotional video for Derbyshire County Council:

Rik and Ade filmed their parts in *Hardwicke House* during the summer months too. Even as it was being shot, the producers were pushing this sitcom as something controversial. Headlines in the local papers around this time said things like 'Terror Of The Schools, The Young Ones Set Up A Class War', and 'School For Scoundrels', even though the two only made an appearance in one episode (that was never aired). It would be a furore that would continue to be stoked for the rest of the year.

Rik took to the stage alone at the end of October 22nd and 23rd) in Frimley Green at the Lakeside Cabaret Club, for a show billed as *Is It 'Kevin' Or 'Rik'? It's RIK MAYALL (plus support show, orchestra and disco)*. Just a few days before this, Frank Carson did a show here called *It's The Way He Tells 'Em*.

In the same month, the Dangerous Brothers were back on screens as *Saturday Almost Live* aired for a repeat run.

Luckily for Ade, this coincided with the publication of his book, *How To Be A Complete Bastard*, which was plugged in an article in the *Daily Mirror*, which also announced the imminent arrival of a new sitcom.

A few days later, Channel Four announced that Rik would be having sex with Paula Yates, or at least talking about sex with her on her new chat show (Reading Evening Post, 17th October 1986). The interview may never have been conducted, and certainly was never broadcast (maybe because it was Too. Damn. SEXY).

At the beginning of November, Rik and Ade reunited in the Oxford Road Studios in Manchester, to begin the filming of *Filthy, Rich And Catflap*. They were joined once more by Nigel Planer, and other faces from *Saturday Live*, including Harry Enfield and Chris Barrie. They would return to the studios fortnightly until the series was in the can.

They took some time away on the 9th November though, to get on stage as Bad News alongside Iron Maiden for a charity gig at the Hammersmith Odeon. Gill Pringle interviewed the band for the *Mirror*:

'"Six showed up for our show at this year's heavy metal festival at Castle Donington," says Vim, while intently picking his nose. "It was great. We had lots of bottles chucked

*at us and none our instruments worked.
Our van broke down and the tent collapsed."
The group claim to have blown fellow heavy
metal stars, Def Leppard, Ossie Osborne and
The Scorpions right off the stage. "They just
couldn't compete," says ace guitarist Den,
who is 37 years old and pretends to be 20.'*

(DAILY MIRROR, 3RD NOVEMBER 1986)

In mid-December, Ade returned to *Wogan*, armed with a bag of explosives which he threatened to use to blow up Terry with if his questions got boring. Terry asks about *Filthy Rich And Catflap*, Ade manages to squeeze in a few lines from the series, and they skirt playfully around the title of his book. All before there's a rather large explosion. Before the year's end, Harold MacMillan passed away, the first case of Mad Cow Disease was diagnosed, and the Guinness shares scandals continued alongside the privatisation of British Gas. If you see Sid, tell him.

1987

Another sub-zero cold snap announced the new year, and on the 7th January Ralph Filthy, Richie Rich, and Edward Catflap burst onto our screens. The show had a full page write up in that week's *Radio Times*.

'They are still perhaps best known to lovers of

While the cast and producers were keen to shrug off *The Young Ones*, the series suffered from unfavourable comparisons to the earlier show, even though Paul Jackson and others were at pains to point out it was a more traditional sitcom. When Ben Elton was the subject of a *South Bank Show* in 1989, he said this:

'Filthy was conceptually a big step forward. I still absolutely adore the idea of this rabid fame-junkie who is desperate, desperate to do anything – read the links on TV-AM ... just desperate for it ... perhaps if I have one regret about Filthy, which I think is actually very funny, is perhaps that we shouted a tiny bit much, put in one too many fart gags, which meant that people could say 'oh, it's only shouting and fart gags'. But I felt that gave it a tremendous vigour, and a tremendous pace.'

At the time, Nick Smurthwaite, writing in *The Stage* (22nd January 1987), accused Ben of throwing the scripts together on the back of a beer mat, and opines that any comedy show with more than two fart gags belongs on children's TV. Elsewhere, Moira Martingale asked:

> '*Does this really reflect the lifestyle of young people nowadays? And if so, might it be a pointer to why our society is so violent?*'

(LIVERPOOL ECHO, 9TH JANUARY 1987)

I've got a lot of time for this show. It's far from perfect, but it's very funny, features some great performances, and skewers its subject well. I didn't see it at the time, and only discovered it in the 90s when it was released on VHS, and it provides an interesting and important bridge between *The Young Ones* and *Bottom*, both stylistically and tonally.

Meanwhile, he PR people had spent their time over the summer and autumn priming the papers with stories about a hard-hitting, controversial new sitcom about school teachers, featuring the anarchic boys from *The Young Ones*. *Hardwicke House*, or the School For Scoundrels, as they would have us believe, aired as a double-length episode with the second one the next day (24-25th Feb), in an unsuitable evening slot. Given that so much effort had been spent on pushing the series as so controversial, it was no surprise that it was received as such.

> *'Schools Out To Shock – A new comedy series about a chaotic comprehensive – which makes St Trinian's and Grange Hill look like kid's stuff – is set to shock parents all over Britain.'*

(DERBY DAILY TELEGRAPH, 20TH FEBRUARY 1987)

Central pulled the rest of the series, and it was never shown again. In the fallout some papers claimed the company had wiped the tapes, even as they denied this was the case.

> *'Hardwicke House Tapes Destroyed – Shock order to 'wipe out' show leaves Central counting the cost. The row over the controversial series Hardwicke House raged on this week when a senior Central executive revealed that the company had been forced to destroy all traces of the series.'*

(ANGELA THOMAS, THE STAGE, 9TH JULY 1987)

> *'Sir, I feel a real spoilsport doing this, but I have to tell you that Angela Thomas' 'exclusive' – isn't actually true. It wasn't true when The Sun carried it a few weeks ago, and it isn't true now. Publishing conspiracy theories may be fun, but checking them is better. Keith Smith, Controller of Public Affairs, Central Television.'*

All this meant that the episode featuring Rik and Ade wasn't seen until it was uploaded in full to YouTube.

Rik has a cameo role in the fifth episode of the first series of *French And Saunders*, which was on BBC Two on the 6th April. He may have been filming *Eat The Rich* during the spring too.

Meanwhile, Adrian was flexing his directing muscles, this time away from the *Comic Strip*. He directed two music videos for Squeeze's album *Babylon And On*. In the first, released in July, the band performs in a surreal, Dali-inspired world, full of weird imagery, and wonderful optical illusions. The second, for *853-5937*, wouldn't be released until February the following year, and this one sees the band inside a telephone.

Around this time (Marks and Gran date it as the end of 1985), Rik met the writers Laurence Marks and Maurice Gran at a comedy symposium in Cheltenham. He asked them to write something for him, and they took his number, but never called him. Two months later, the writers were on Wogan to talk about their experience of writing in America, and Rik was there that night too (to plug *Living Doll*). He said 'you were supposed to phone me you bastards!'. So they took him out for lunch.

> *'He challenged us to create for him a funny, new, grown-up character, the polar opposite of the spotty, beret-wearing, right-on student*

'Wrick' he had created for himself in The Young Ones ... He explained that he enjoyed roles that let him express the dark side of his personality. "I like to cheat and lie. I don't mind the occasional murder. I'd be good at murder. Greed is good. Stealing. Arson ... Oh, and lots of sex." Rik continued describing such an abhorrent individual that we feared that it would be a difficult sell, until after a mouthful of peach Melba one of us said, "So you want to play a Conservative member of parliament." He laughed hysterically. We had connected.'

(SHOOTING THE PILOT, LAURENCE MARKS AND MAURICE GRAN, PG 81-82)

At the same symposium in Cheltenham, Marks and Gran had also met the Head Of Comedy for Yorkshire Television, Vernon Lawrence, and become friends with him. He was a fan of Mayall's, thinking him the best thing since Leonard Rossiter, ever since seeing him in *The Government Inspector*. So they offered this new idea to Lawrence, and he snapped it up.

They began writing the pilot, then the series, as more national assets were sold off to line rich pockets, as Edwina Curry declared that 'good Christians won't get AIDS', as Cynthia Payne was acquitted of controlling prostitutes at her London home, as six Nazi war criminals were alleged to be living in the UK, as the Pound was riding high, as prescription charges rose, as IRA bombs exploded, as Van Gogh's Sunflowers sold for £24.5 million, as a Tory MP was charged with gross indecency, and as Margaret Thatcher called and won another General Election.

So, as Rik stepped into Studio 4 at Television Centre, in August, Alan B'Stard arrived fully-formed, full of vitriol, and fully representative of the real world. His performance was so incandescent that it would burn into the country's collective retina, and leave itself there for years to come.

The same couldn't be said for the *Comic Strip's* second feature film, *Eat The Rich*, which was released on August the 17th, and is now ranked by Time Out as the 49th greatest cinema flop. Both Rik and Ade have small roles in the film.

At the end of August, Rik took some time off from *The New Statesman* recordings to join Adrian and the others on stage as Bad News at the Reading Festival, which served as a marker for their upcoming autumn tour, taking in Leicester, Edinburgh, Manchester, Bristol and others, before culminating in a double date at the Hammersmith Odeon.

On the 2nd October, the band were caught lip-synching on *Wogan*, as they performed *Bohemian Rhapsody*, which Vim also claimed he wrote, and Queen stole. At one point, Colin's wig comes off, revealing Rik is still sporting Alan B'Stard's haircut, and as the segment comes to a close, Rik blurts that he will be playing at Blazer's in Windsor the following night.

In December, Rik appeared in a Yorkshire Television public awareness film, dressed as Alan B'Stard, which was clearly shot on the office set of *The New Statesman*, in front of a live audience. He does his ear trick, and then announces a helpline for anyone struggling at Christmas.

1988

At the turn of 1988, on January 3rd to be precise, Margaret Thatcher became the longest serving British Prime Minister of the 20th Century, in spite of everything that alternative comedy had done to try and bring her down. Rowan Atkinson officially launched the next *Comic Relief*, which meant that Rik and Ade were recording their contributions. Ade filmed some documentary inserts about disability in Britain, and Rik shot a *New Statesman* special, in which he channels Rick for one delightful moment of inspired comedy. The show on 5th February would go on to raise £15 million and was watched by a large audience.

> *'The top of the chart this week has been completely transformed by the Comic Relief broadcast from BBC1 on Friday. This extravaganza proved tremendously popular, attracting an average audience of more than 10.6 million viewers for nearly seven hours. The highest recorded audience of the evening*

was for Wood, Walters And Wise (nearly 16.6 million viewers) which, together with four other 'programmes' took a well deserved place in the top 10.'

(BROADCAST, 4TH MARCH 1988)

And while *George's Marvellous Medicine* was enjoying a repeat, and raising the ire of the squares, it was announced that Rik would join Stephen Fry and John Sessions on stage in a revival of Simon Gray's play *The Common Pursuit*. It would have a short run in Watford at the Palace Theatre at the beginning of March, before transferring to the West End at the Phoenix.

'The performances, all that little bit theatrically heightened, are thoroughly absorbing in a play which gives civilised enjoyment yet at the same time has something important, if occasionally depressing, to say.'

(PETER HEPPLE, THE STAGE, 21ST APRIL 1988)

The cast appeared on *Wogan* to push the West End preview show on 28th March, where Rik and John Gordon Sinclair admit to their Sex Competition, and leave the audience screaming (sort of).

Gray would later adapt the play for *Screen Two*, with Stephen Fry returning to the same role. Fry also makes reference to the play in an episode of his excellent Radio Four show *Saturday Night Fry*, which was aired around the time the play was on at The Phoenix.

March was a busy time on TV screens for both Rik and Ade, as the new series of *The Comic Strip Presents ...* began airing on Channel 4, including them alongside Peter Cook in the now-classic *Mr Jolly Lives Next Door*, and the return of the band in *More Bad News*. As well as a joint appearance in *The Strike*, Ade also appeared on his own in *The Yob*.

Over on BBC Two, Adrian popped up in a couple of episodes of the second series of *French And Saunders* (doop be doopee doo). But aside from a repeat run of *Happy Families*, the duo were absent from screens for the rest of the year.

And let's not overlook the most astonishing thing of the spring and summer of 1988. A cinephile's dream. A completist's wet dream.

Management Accountancy – The Movie.

This was a corporate recruitment video, showcased around the country by Michael Page Partnership, starring Rowan Atkinson, Jan Francis, and Adrian Edmondson. The company screened the video at their offices and on campuses around the UK and Ireland. The company also produced *Head Start*, in a similar vein, featuring Mel Smith and Griff Rhys Jones.

Rik also made a corporate video in 1988, but his was for John Cleese's Video Arts production company. *Managing Problem People: Behavioral Skills For Leaders* was directed by Charles Crichton (who later directed *A Fish Called Wanda*), and was written by Stephen Fry. It also starred Cleese,

Dawn French, Fry, Geoffrey Palmer, Patricia Hodge, Jennifer Saunders, and Emma Thompson.

In September, Adrian was on location filing his role as Simon Knowles in an episode of *Press Gang*, before he got the band back together for a few dates in November and December.

1989

1989 would mark Margaret Thatcher's tenth year as Prime Minister, but would also see the first challenge to her leadership of the Tory party, when Anthony Meyer stood against her in a contest. He went on to lose this, but 60 MPs voted against her. Nonetheless, arch Thatcherite Alan Beresford B'Stard returned to ITV screens on the 15th January, and he would be shot at the end of the series. Perhaps everyone saw the writing on the wall, but the character would survive this attempt on his life (orchestrated by himself, obviously), and outlive his heroine in terms of time in Parliament.

> '*The New Statesman was the most exhausting show we have ever written. Having finished one series we didn't have the energy to imagine ever embarking upon another one. Our solution was to kill off Alan ... If we could leave him dead in the last show of the last scene of the last episode, we could breathe a sigh of relief. But Yorkshire*

Television always had other ideas. They would make us revive him ... And yes, it was also the most rewarding series we ever wrote.'

(SHOOTING THE PILOT, PG 83)

Perhaps given the success of his turn on *Jackanory* (apparently he doubled the ratings), Rik began narrating *Grim Tales* for Childrens ITV in April, telling twelve different stories in consecutive weeks. The show later transferred to Channel 4 for its second series of ten episodes.

'I love the stories of the Brothers Grimm ... they are so colourful and I remember my own father used to read me similar stories. Now I am having to carry on the tradition with my own children, Rosemary and Sidney. I really enjoy storytelling. For me, reading Grim Tales was a bit like doing a one-man show.'

(SANDWELL EVENING MAIL, 6TH APRIL 1989)

Spring also saw Rik go on tour.

'I'm going out on the road with a new show. Ben Elton's expressed an interest in coming along, but then there'd be a battle over who's top of the bill and we don't want to turn into Tarby and Lynchy!'

(FIRST CLASS MAYALL, RECORD MIRROR, 4TH FEBRUARY 1989)

To prevent the clash, he decided to tour with Andy De La Tour instead. They did a few dates in March and April (including The Hawth in Crawley, and Worthing Pavilions), before ending the year with dozens of dates in November and December.

> *'His detractors call him vulgar and degenerate, his fans describe him as wacky and zany but love him or loathe him Rik Mayall touches a chord with a large proportion of today's young people. This was proved when he had no difficulty in filling the Hawth, Crawley, last week. With its roots set firmly in the kindergarten, his show began with a sequence of carefully modulated raspberries blown from behind the curtain. Modesty is not in his vocabulary and his entrance is heralded by the Hallelujah chorus from Handel's Messiah ... He sets himself up as a metaphor for style and coolness and his act is the unravelling of that central conceit. The 80 minute long show is punctured by his antics. He skips and jumps about pulling faces like a hyper active child trying to show just how silly he can be.'*

(SIMON HOLDEN, THE STAGE, 27TH APRIL 1989)

On 3rd November, Rik and Andy were both guests on *One Hour With Jonathan Ross*. Field reporter Roland Rivron had a camera live at the Alexandra Theatre in Birmingham, where he went into the dressing room with Andy, and then out onto the stage during Rik's set, much to the live audience's delight. Ross then interviewed Rik via video.

Psst – The Really Useful Guide To Alcohol was a blend of comedy and public information, and aired on BBC One in May and June. Rik is in a sketch in the 15th May episode, while many more comedy faces pop up across the series, including Harry Enfield, Rowan Atkinson, Helen Lederer, Smith And Jones, Norman Lovett, and Patricia Routledge.

Sometime during the year, Adrian could be seen hovering in the air, playing some sort of magical being, while flogging us the virtues of renting a telly from Granada Rentals. He signs off the advert by asking us 'how switched on can you get?'.

On the 18th September, the Terrence Higgins Trust staged its second AIDS benefit at the Sadler's Wells Theatre. Written and directed by Stephen Fry, with additional material by Richard Curtis, the show featured a host of performers including Adrian Edmondson, who came on to tell his joke, and then later demonstrate some safe, and unsafe, sex positions with Robbie Coltrane, Dawn French, and Stephen Fry.

Also in September, over three nights at the Cambridge Theatre, comedy stars gathered for Amnesty's *The Secret Policeman's Biggest Ball*. This fundraiser reunited Peter Cook and Dudley Moore. Adrian again appeared on stage, this time as Michaelangelo (opposite Cleese's Pope), and the whole thing was released on video in October.

Elsewhere in October, the writers of *The New Statesman*, Laurence Marks and Maurice Gran presented their sitcom about the dystopian future that Thatcherism and Rupert Murdoch were destined to bring about. *Snakes And Ladders* is set in 1999, and stars John Gordon Sinclair, alongside Ade. This single series for Channel 4 aired the day after the writers' BBC One sitcom *Birds Of A Feather*, and may have slipped off of people's radars.

> *'The company and writers could have played safe and churned out one more soft-centred sit-com but that's only marking time and here they are taking risks. And it works.'*

(THE STAGE, 12TH OCTOBER 1989)

Rik makes a cameo in the seventh, and final, episode.

He also made yet another remarkable, show-stealing cameo in *Blackadder Goes Forth* the same week, as he reprised his role as Flashheart, complete with sexy leather coat. He recorded the episode just a month before on the 17th September, and this time he was joined on set and on screen by Ade as the Red Baron. Rowan Atkinson describes this as the performance of Rik's career (The True History of the Black Adder, pg 307), and it was watched by 11.95 million viewers, almost the same number as watched *Birds Of A Feather*. It's fair to say the alternative set was rather more mainstream now.

Before the year was out, Adrian made some on camera contributions to the Channel 4 documentary about Tommy Cooper. *Just Like That!* aired on the 28th December, and also featured The Goons, Lenny Henry, and Patricia Hodge, among many others.

1990

When the calendar clicked over into 1990, the first MORI poll of the year showed Labour with a commanding 12 point lead. Ambulance crews went on strike, rebel cricketers tried to play a match in South Africa, and a hurricane ripped through the country killing 39 people. Labour's lead in those polls would grow throughout the year, and rising discontent over the Poll Tax would erupt into riots and mass demonstrations. The local elections saw big gains for Kinnock's party – the writing was on the wall for Thatcher ...
So the right wing press was making every effort to throw out as many distractions as possible.
After successfully rising from the dead in the *Who Shot Alan B'Stard?* special on 14th January, Rik resumed his tour with Andy De La Tour. In the middle of March, *The Sun* newspaper, and other local rags, reported that Rik told a joke that had been part of his set throughout the tour in the past year, and were in predictable uproar about it (it was about being locked in a fridge).

'He immediately realised what he had said and apologised "unreservedly" to the packed

Rik quickly apologised, and said he would never do the joke again.

To their credit, the *Birmingham Mail* followed up the story the next day, reporting that during his subsequent show at the Royal Shakespeare Theatre in Stratford, the joke had been cut, and giving the whole show a big thumbs up in their review.

It would be remarkably interesting timing if Adrian had been on set at this time filming his new *Screen One* play *News Hounds*, about the unscrupulous behaviour of tabloid journalists. In another collaboration with Les Blair, Ade played the role of Phil Burke, a boorish predator with no moral compass, alongside Alison Steadman and Christopher Fulford. Writing about the experience of filming this, Ade recalls the months long rehearsal period as incredibly enjoyable and beneficial, and describes his week shadowing hacks at the *Daily Star*.

News Hounds was broadcast on the 2nd September on BBC One, and in the same month Ade made a cameo on Rita Rudner's BBC Two sketch and stand up show.

A large part of Adrian's year was spent on stage in the West End, when he played Brad in a revival of the *Rocky Horror Show*. Joining his was Tim McInnerny, and as a small promotional opportunity, Ade appeared on a late night ITV show called *Books By My Bedside* at the end of October.

One of his choices of reading material instigates a fascinating chat with the host Brough Scott, as Adrian reveals he's currently reading the script book of *Steptoe And Son*.

> *'I started reading this because I'm working with Rik Mayall at the moment, we're writing a new sitcom, and I thought I'd look at some of the greats … It's a sitcom called Bottom, which is about two men who are at the bottom, which is a kind of similarity between this.'*

He also mentions Hancock, and it's clear that the two took great inspiration from both these earlier shows. The timing of this confirms that they began writing the full series after Rik had filmed his role in *Drop Dead Fred* in Minneapolis in August and September of this year. Before that, in July, Rik had been filming a small indie film called *Little Noises*, starring alongside Crispin Glover in a story about artistic theft.

Adrian also describes the evolution of his writing partnership with Rik. He explains that it used to be confrontational.

> *'We used to have a very tortuous time writing because we always used to do each other down, and say "that's not funny, come up with something funny". But now we've sort of relaxed and we're into the mood. We've actually worked out that it works better if I'm sitting down and he's standing up.'*

Years later, on Triple J Radio in Australia, Rik confirmed that he was the pacer, and Ade was the typer. Ade quipped 'I don't listen to anything he says, I just write the script while he's in the room.' Now watch *Bottom* and note how often Eddie is sitting while Richie is on his feet pacing around.

This change in the writing dynamic coincides with the pair's most fecund period together, and I can't imagine that's a coincidence.

If they are writing the full series of *Bottom* in the autumn of 1990, then it puts pay to the persistent bit of trivia that they came up with the idea for the show whilst performing *Waiting For Godot*. The timing of this could never have been correct anyway, not least because they had already written and filmed the pilot of *Bottom* by this time.

They shot the episode that would become *Contest* on the 24th June at Television Centre. So at least one slice of Rik and Ade's *Bottom* was already sitting on a shelf.

And they're writing as Thatcher's time in office is coming to an end, just as Geoffrey Howe makes his devastating resignation speech to the House, which sparks a new leadership contest in the Tory party.

Something for which Marks and Gran didn't quite have the same serendipity. They had to do a lot of rewriting for the third series of *The New Statesman*, just as Thatcher was defenestrated, ready for the new series to hit screens in January of 1991.

> *'We always said we wanted B'Stard to be around after Thatcher had gone. On November 22, 1990, our wish came true.'*

(SHOOTING THE PILOT, PG 86)

While on an episode of *Wogan*, Rik recalls:

> *'The last time we did [The New Stateseman] … We'd just finished all the scripts, we recorded one, and Thatcher resigned. So all the scripts were out of date, over night. The cow!'*

(9TH SEPT 1991)

He continues that he got so happy that night he fell down the stairs and dislocated his shoulder, which gave them a three week respite to do some re-writes.

Adrian would have been filming his part in *The Pope Must Die* towards the end of this year too, somewhere in Yugoslavia. The film was originally designed as a three-part mini-series in 1988, which Channel 4 cancelled in the midst of another press furore.

> *'Channel 4 has scrapped plans for three programmes which would have satirised the Papacy. Lawyers have advised that the series from The Comic Strip group of comedians presents too many potential legal problems ... The series was due to star Alexei Sayle ... as 'Pope Dave the First', and would also have featured comedians Robbie Coltrane, Dawn French and Jennifer Saunders. The programmes would have been in the form of a parody of an American mini-series, which portrayed a modern-day Pope and his rule across two continents. "It's a big disappointment for me," Sayle said yesterday. "It would have been my first chance of a major leading role." The channel has decided instead to commission another programme from The Comic Strip. 'Five Go to Hell' is to be set in a corrupt South American country, and is a parody of Enid Blyton's 'Famous Five' books and characters. The 'Five' meet up again after an absence of 20 years in South America.'*

(OBSERVER, 18TH SEPTEMBER 1988)

Five Go To Hell was never made, and Peter

Richardson, incensed by the shelving, took the *Comic Strip* to BBC Two. The scripts were reworked, with two of them being repurposed into the *Spaghetti Hoops* and *Oxford* episodes of the new BBC series, while the main idea was produced as the movie by Palace Pictures.

1991

The big three US television networks refused to run commercials for the film, and London Transport, echoing their decision from a decade before, refused to run adverts on their buses (LA Times, 25h Aug 1991).

Nonetheless, the film opened across 170 screens in the UK in June of 1991, with a limited release in the States on the same number of screens in September.

Drop Dead Fred on the other hand, opened in the States in May of 1991, and later here in the UK in October.

Rik chatted with Triple J Radio in Australia a few years later about how he was cast in the movie. 'Two Americans had seen *The Young Ones*, and they came over with a script about me being a crap policeman in Yorkshire. It was not a very good script, so I said 'no' … and they said "ah go on Rik, we wanna write something for you", so they wrote that instead.' Those two writers were Carlos Davis and Anthony Fingleton.

In March, Adrian promoted *Comic Relief* in promos

for the BBC, in which he attempts to give himself a red nose, in increasingly violent ways.

Thus, 1991 was a busy year for the Hammersmith Hard Men. They continued writing the first series of *Bottom* as war raged in the Gulf, recession raged in the UK, unemployment continued to rise, IRA mortars hit Downing Street, and interest rates sky-rocketed. It must have felt rather reminiscent of the early 1980s, and there were the first stirrings of the Back To Basics nonsense, in an effort to distract everyone from the current problems by harking back to a fictional time of Anglo bliss.

Together they stepped into the studio at Television Centre, and began filming the remaining five episodes of *Bottom's* first series.

As part of his promotions for *Drop Dead Fred*, and serendipitously *Bottom* too, Rik rubbed belly buttons with Gloria Hunniford, when she sat in for Terry on *Wogan*, on the 9th September. He came on to a rendition of *Pictures At Exhibition*, looking devilishly handsome even with his long Richie hair, and told a story about how the movie's crew were banned from an art gallery. He also recalls a party thrown by French and Saunders which screened his naked bottom on a loop throughout. They show a brief clip from *Smells*, and Rik reveals that he has been rehearsing *Waiting For Godot* all afternoon with Ade.

The play, directed by Les Blair, opened for previews at the Queen's Theatre on 23rd September, and opening night was on the 30th. In a review that could easily have been about *Bottom*, Peter Hepple said:

> *'What or who are these two derelicts waiting for? It doesn't really matter. They are waiting for something to turn up, for their present condition to get better. And as they do so, they make the time pass, by mock arguments and abuse, by silly games, by sleeping and eating, by staying out of trouble and by trying to retain their identities.'*

(THE STAGE, 10TH OCTOBER 1991)

At the end of the year, Edmondson himself told Jonathan Ross that 'our writing is a bit Beckettian'. Talking to *Box Office*, Les Blair said 'I think a lot of what they do comes out of Beckett originally. The fascinating thing for me has been watching them translate our intellectual conversations about what each section of the play means, into the sort of physicality that they bring to it.'
In the *Radio Times* the week that *Bottom* began, there was an interview with Rik and Ade.

> *'As Edmondson says, "These days we've lost all interest in popular culture. Bottom has nothing to do with pop music or people under 30. And there's nothing fashionable in it – hopefully." "We're more interested in the things that have always been there," says Mayall. "In Bottom, the gas man comes round from the gas board. We have postal*

*orders, post offices and telephone boxes.
These are things that have lasted since before
1955 – before Elvis really got going and
rock 'n' roll started. But all that stuff didn't
happen for these guys. Like it doesn't happen
for us any more. We're too old."'*

(RADIO TIMES, 14TH-20TH SEPTEMBER 1991)

*'Richie and Eddie are out of step with one
each other and the world around them, but
still yearn for a better class of life.'*

(NEWCASTLE EVENING CHRONICLE, 17TH SEPTEMBER 1991)

And so, as riots broke out in the North East, unemployment hit its highest level for years, Labour lagged in the polls, and Major planned a snap general election, BBC Two showed everyone Rik and Ade's *Bottom*.

LINE

1990

24 – 25 July: Studio recording for *Contest* (TC6)

1991

4 June – Filming of Opening Titles in Hammersmith

13 - 14 June: Studio recording for *Smells* (TC1)

20 - 21 June: Studio recording for *Apocalypse* (TC8)

27 - 28 June: Studio recording for *'S Up* (TC8)

4 - 5 July: Studio recording for *Gas* (TC1)

12 July: Studio recording for *Accident* (TC1)

17 September: First broadcast of **Smells**

24 September: First broadcast of **Gas**

1 October: First broadcast of **Contest**

8 October: First broadcast of **Apocalypse**

15 October: First broadcast of **'S Up**

29 October: First broadcast of **Accident**

1992

10 – 11 May: Studio recording for *'S Out* (TC8)

17 – 18 May: Studio recording for *Culture* (TC8)

24 – 25 May: Studio recording for *Burglary* (TC1)

2 – 3 July: Studio recording for *Parade* (TC3)

9 – 10 July: Studio recording for *Holy* (TC3)

16 – 17 July: Studio recording for *Digger* (TC1)

1 October: First broadcast of **Digger**

8 October: First broadcast of **Culture**

15 October: First broadcast of **Burglary**

22 October: First broadcast of **Parade**

29 October: First broadcast of **Holy**

5 December: *Bottom* wins Best New TV Comedy at the *British Comedy Awards*

1993

14 April: *Bottom: Live* tour begins at Rhyl New Pavilion

18 – 19 June: *Bottom: Live* filmed at the Southampton Mayflower

6 July: *Bottom Live* tour ends at Birmingham Symphony Hall

27 September: **Bottom: Live** released on home video

15 November: ***Bottom: The Scripts*** published

1994

27 – 28 September: Studio recording for *Dough*

29 September: ***Bottom: More Scripts*** published

4 – 5 October: Studio recording for *Terror*

11 – 12 October: Studio recording for *Carnival*

25 – 26 October: Studio recording for *Break* and *Finger* (pre-record only)

2 November: Studio recording for *Finger*

8 – 9 November: Studio recording for *Hole*

1995

6 January: First broadcast of ***Hole***

13 January: First broadcast of ***Terror***

20 January: First broadcast of ***Break***

27 January: First broadcast of ***Dough***

3 February: First broadcast of ***Finger***

10 February: First broadcast of ***Carnival***

10 April: First broadcast of ***'S Out***

18 September: *Bottom Live: The Big Number 2 Tour* begins at Bristol Hippodrome

9 – 10 October: *Bottom Live: The Big Number 2 Tour* filmed at Oxford Apollo

6 November: ***Bottom Live: The Big Number 2 Tour***
released on home video

20 December: *Bottom Live: The Big Number 2 Tour*
ends at Nottingham Royal Centre

1996

4 November: ***Bottom: Fluff*** released on home video

1997

13 January: *Bottom Live 3: Hooligan's Island* begins
at Nottingham Royal Centre

17 – 22 March: *Bottom Live 3: Hooligan's Island*
filmed at Bristol Hippodrome

22 March: *Bottom Live 3: Hooligan's Island* ends at
Bristol Hippodrome

27 October: ***Bottom Live 3: Hooligan's Island***
released on home video

1999

3 December – ***Guest House Paradiso*** opens in UK
cinemas

2001

17 September: *Bottom 2001: An Arse Oddity* begins
at Sunderland Empire

8 October: *Bottom 2001: An Arse Oddity* filmed at Nottingham Royal Centre

19 November: ***Bottom 2001: An Arse Oddity*** released on home video

30 November: *Bottom 2001: An Arse Oddity* ends at Bournemouth BIC

2003

3 October: *Bottom 2003: Weapons Grade Y-Fronts* begins at Glasgow Clyde Auditorium

28 – 30 October*: Bottom 2003: Weapons Grade Y-Fronts* filmed at Cliffs Pavilion

24 November: ***Bottom 2003: Weapons Grade Y-Fronts*** released on home video

11 December: *Bottom 2003: Weapons Grade Y-Fronts* ends at Wolverhampton Civic Hall

SMELLS

Written by Adrian Edmondson and Rik Mayall
Produced and Directed by Ed Bye

Duration
29m24s

Recording Dates
Thursday 13th – Friday 14th June 1991
Transmission Date
Tuesday 17th September 1991 at 9.00pm

Cast
Richard Richard – Rik Mayall
Edward Hitler – Adrian Edmondson
Mr Sex – Kevin McNally
Woman At Bar – Harriet Thorpe
Woman's Husband – Clive Mantle
Landlord – Lee Cornes
Kate – Cindy Shelley
Jenny – Carla Mendonca
Young Man At Window – Timothy Welton
Young Woman At Window – Yvonne Burne

BARB Ratings
6.4m (55th/2nd)

Radio Times Blurb

'A new black comedy series written by and

starring Adrian Edmondson and Rik Mayall who shot to cult status in "The Young Ones", the anarchic sit-com about four weird students living in a festering flat. They went on to do "Filthy, Rich and Catflap" and "The Comic Strip Presents" series. Rik Mayall starred in "The New Statesman", recently repeated on Channel 4. The title of this new series apparently owes less to Britain's famous lavatorial-level of humour, and more to the fact that the two main characters are bottom of the heap, but with aspirations to better themselves. Rik Mayall and Adrian Edmondson are currently rehearsing a new production of Samuel Beckett's "Waiting for Godot", which opens in London later this month. Richie and Eddie set out to improve their sex lives, which shouldn't be difficult as sex is something they haven't experienced for a while.'

Synopsis

Richie and Eddie come home from the pub, disappointed that their vile machinations were badly-received by the patrons. In a funk, they compose a Lonely Hearts advert for the classified column of the *Hammersmith Bugle*. In doing so, Richie comes across an advert for a pheromone spray, and so the next day, they pay a visit to the local, seedy sex shop.

Their confidence bolstered by their new spray,

they get ready for another night out, but it descends into a full blown brawl in the bathroom. They call a truce, and apply the spray, which has a peculiar effect upon Eddie.

They make a nuisance of themselves in the Lamb And Flag, annoying everyone in there, until two women, Kate and Jenny, reluctantly agree to a drink. Richie stupidly takes this as a sign, and he takes Eddie to the toilets to buy some condoms. Upon their return to the bar, they find that Kate and Jenny have taken the opportunity to move, which angers Richie, who becomes rude and indignant. Stoned on the spray now though, Eddie begins to 'seduce' Richie – and it all ends with a punch to the face.

Reviews

'Bottom is huge! Within two days of smells, the first episode of Edmondson and Mayall's new BBC2 sitcom, it had already passed into folklore. An ironmongers in West Hampstead had a pair of pliers in the window with a notice about "essential personal grooming." ... The slapstick fights, exploding sets, gross physical appetites and scatological bathroom humour that plumbs previously uncharted depths do give a familiar Young Ones feel to Bottom. Eddie and Richie, though, are not merely Vyv and Wick decayed. This pair of social and sexual inadequates have a pathos that undercuts

the frenetic grossness and are firmly rooted in British comedy tradition. Mayall's frustrated virgin seemed almost shaded by Hancock in his more reflective moments and Edmondson, whose trick of perfectly timed literal observation is already emerging as a great running gag, surely recalled Eric Morecambe ... Bottom made me laugh out loud more than anything on screens in years.'

(BARBARA HOLLOWAY, THE STAGE, 3RD OCTOBER 1991)

'When Rik Mayall wiped his nose on Gloria Hunniford's sleeve to plug his new comedy Bottom last week, I had a little smile. Sorry Gloria. Shockingly horrible oafs can sometimes be funny. Look at Rab C. Nesbit. But the first flash of Bottom, a sort of boys' cartoon, was only about as clever as a bogey on a lady's sleeve. Rik Mayall and Ade Edmondson are a couple of rancid and randy bachelors who share a flat, a taste for fry-ups, alcohol and a desperate desire for sex (with anything female that breathes). A bit like every man you ever met, really. On Tuesday they bought a spray from a sex shop to ensure women would find them irresistible and "death by sex" was on the cards. Sadly not even Abby from Howards Way who was unaccountably drinking in their local pub, could bear them long enough to say "push

off". Apart from noting how fat Rik had become, I laughed only once - when Ade ate a slab of lard.'

(HILLARY KINGSLEY, DAILY MIRROR, 21ST SEPTEMBER 1991)

'Why Bottom is tops with viewers - The worrying thing about Bottom running again on BBC2 is that when you wipe off all the muck you get a pretty clear picture of a lot of low-life chaps you might know or even be in reality. In the first episode we see Richie Richard and Eddie Hitler (Rik Mayall and Ade Edmondson) reduced to buying pheromone perfume in the vain hope of wooing a woman only to try thrusting their attentions on a pair of lesbians in a pub. Unemployed deadbeats at the bottom of the heap, Richie is a sex-starved hypocritical virgin and Eddie an amoral devious entrepreneur The odd couple live together in a ruinous bachelor pad and seem to lead a lifestyle not far removed from that of the Young Ones characters that launched the actors' careers "Ade and I are still doing what we like best Rik (33) admitted "It's just what makes us laugh". They weren't the only ones, for despite a flood of complaints about the obscenity, foul language, and violence in the series, Bottom was the tops when it was first shown last Autumn, pulling in a regular

audience of 6.2 million, to make it the most watched comedy on BBC2 that year. "Maybe it's because they are both crafty, yet stupid" mused Rik, who co-wrote the series with Ade. "Their moments of sanity are eclipsed by other moments of almost clinical insanity and irrational behaviour". "Richie and Eddie both want to climb out of their rut, even if it means standing on each other's head to get up, but they are always beaten because they are so out of step with each other and reality as a whole which is just how we like it!"'

(ROSSENDALE FREE PRESS, 19TH JUNE 1992)

Guff

Right from the opening title sequence, I was sold. That bleak music, the world going on around, and in spite of, our hapless main characters - the sheer drabness of it all leant itself to that title.
Bottom.
These two are there. Rock bottom, with nowhere else to go, and no-one else to be with.
Ed Bye did a masterful job shooting those titles (John Else was the cameraman), and the music by the Bum Notes is so evocative that the melancholy is palpable. So when Richie bursts into tears, well, it's pitch perfect.
Bye's excellent direction continues throughout the episode, starting with the first shot, leading us into the drawing room from the hallway. Bleak rain lashes at the window, and there's a vertical

depth to the set that's rarely seen in sitcoms. We can look down on the decaying shop fronts below. Rik times his first gag to coincide with turning on the light, and we're off.

The whole set is dressed to reflect the tone - drab, dirty walls, board games held together with yellowed Sellotape, dust all around the TV, a single piece of tinsel still dangling in a dank corner, and the cheap, broken 1950s furniture. Even the little Union Flag bag hung up with a grubby colander reflects the theme (there's so much false patriotism ahead, and this little touch sums it up nicely).

And the way our main characters always wear the same clothes - a trick that cartoons pull off, and one *The Young Ones* did too – we can recognise them in silhouette. Eddie's in a suit and tie, wears a hat, even though he has nowhere to go.

The theme of the show unfolds over a long, opening scene, and it's well-stated, and funny throughout. This is a skewering of toxic masculinity and male entitlement just as Laddism was about to take hold of the zeitgeist.

"I mean, just think of all those acres and acres of ladies all lying there saying, 'Come on darling, let's do it' and the bloke's saying, 'No, I don't feel like doing it – the snooker's on.' Well, I could be filling in for him! Providing a service. Could even charge." And instead of addressing their shortcomings (which they do recognise in moments of clarity), they turn instead to trickery, using a pheromone spray like the pick-up-artists they weirdly aspire to be. This was before the internet, and so they head for a grubby, back-alley boutique of ill-repute.

Notice the look of glee on Rik's face just before he reaches up and grabs the dildo in the sex shop. I don't know if he found that in the moment, or it was rehearsed, but he knows that huge laugh is coming.

The pliers scene was pre-recorded, but gets a big reaction from the audience nonetheless, as it was played to them on the monitors.

I worried that the pub scene might feel all wrong these days, but it's actually aged rather well.

Harriet Thorpe is great in a limited role (the women are all rather under-written here, alas), but at least they have some lines, and some agency – albeit not enough. What strikes me most about the misogyny here is how Richie and Eddie are *clearly* the butt of the jokes. Their lines are outdated, outmoded, and played to humiliate themselves.

Ultimately, Richie and Eddie are the victims of their own vile scheming. Eddie overdoses on the pheromones, and makes a pass at Richie, before the obligatory freeze frame mid-cartoon violence.

And then that joyous closing credits sequence, also scored by the Bum Notes.

Nuggets

Smells was the second episode recorded. It was shot in Studio 1 (TC1) at BBC Television Centre. This is the same studio used for *The Two Ronnies*, *I'm Alan Partridge*, *Shooting Stars*, *Fawlty Towers*, many drama series, and so much more including *Noel's House Party* and *Wogan*.

The opening titles were filmed on Tuesday 4th June 1991. They run for approximately 40 seconds (it varies from episode to episode).

The shot in the opening titles, of Richie and Eddie looking through the window that turns out to be a facade, was shot on the building site of what was to become the Coca-Cola building at 1 Queen Caroline Street. It is being built next to Richie and Eddie on the bench.

The bench in the opening titles was located on a traffic island on Hammersmith Bridge Road facing the church, shot from the corner of St Paul's Green and looking down the A4129. A memorial bench to Rik sits in the same spot now, although it has been angled 90 degrees and now faces down Hammersmith Bridge Road rather than facing the park and church. You can see where the camera was placed for the bench shot as the camera zooms out from the window. In the top left corner of the frame, you see the church, and the green.

The music used for the title sequence is *B.B. Blues* by B.B. King, performed by The Bum Notes.

The music used for the closing titles is *Last Night*, and is also performed by The Bum Notes – who also performed all of the instrumental stings (written by Simon Brint).

The Bum Notes are Simon Brint (Leader), Bud Beadle (Sax), Steve Dawson (Trumpet), Martin Elliot (Bass Guitar), Gavin Harrison (Drums), Chris Marshall (Piano), Roddy Matthews (Guitar), and Peter Thomas (Tenor Sax).

When Eddie turns on the TV after they return from the pub at the beginning, we hear the library music *'Murder, Mystery And Suspense'* by Wolfgang Kafer.

The Lamb And Flag pub, whose Landlord is Dick Head, is decorated with boxing paraphernalia, including old bill posters and publicity shots.

Dick Head is credited as Landlord, and named as such in the original script.

The man behind the counter in the shop is called Mr Sex.

Adrian revealed in a web chat with *The Guardian*, that he really ate lard.

Bottom replaced *Rab C Nesbitt* in the schedules, which ended its run the previous week.

Carla Mendonca, who plays Jenny, also appeared in *The Young Ones* episode *Sick*. She later married Clive Mantle, who plays the man at the bar.

Cindy Shelley, who plays Kate, made her television debut in *The Young Ones* episode *Interesting*, and then again in *Flood*.

Other comedy shows airing the same night were *My Two Dads* (Ch4 6pm) – *Happy Days* (Ch4 6.30pm) – *Bilko* (BBC Two – 7.20pm) – *The Fall And Rise Of Reginald Perrin* (BBC One 8pm) – *2point4 Children* (BBC One 8.30pm) – *French Fields* (ITV 8.30pm) – *The Staggering Stories Of Ferdinand De Bargos* (BBC Two 10.10pm).

The local newspaper is called the *Hammersmith Bugle*, which is not a real title. The prop however, is made from the 31st May 1991 edition of the *Richmond Informer*. The front page features an article about Sooty appearing at the local swimming pool, and the main story is about a pensioner who narrowly avoided a falling plane part.

Rik very nearly laughs when he delivers the line 'clenching my buttocks'.

Richie and Eddie seem to be in the middle of a game of *Risk*. Red is winning by a mile. It's been put away by the next day, on top of the cupboard above the organ, along with *Buccaneer* and *Cluedo*.

The shop is called Sex Mart.

The glue Richie uses to glue on his underpants is called Eterno-Gum.

Unseen character, Norman, came round with some sherry and they ended up putting condoms on their heads.

According to a sign on the wall, the Lamb And Flag has a Karaoke Night every Saturday. Except this week it seems.

Ade must have hurt himself when he punches the condom machine – his blow lands so hard it leaves a huge dent.

Richie claims his catalogues flop open on the lingerie page – this bears out when he opens one in *Bottom: Live*.

Script Cuts/Deleted Scenes

A few lines are cut from the script, some for time, and some for more obvious reasons. These include:

- Richie has a moment of clarity wherein he realises his machinations and trickery have deeply dodgy consent issues.
- An argument about who owes what for the taxi fare.
- Some more woodland creature suggestions for the classified ad.
- A testimonial for the pheromone spray in the advert.
- Richie and Eddie expressing alarm at some of the things in the sex shop, including an orange squeezer – and them emulating some grunting noises from other patrons of the shop.
- Richie, indignantly turning down an offer of free pornography from Mr Sex, the man

behind the counter in the shop.

GAS

Written by Adrian Edmondson and Rik Mayall
Produced and Directed by Ed Bye

Duration
29m24s

Recording Dates
Thursday 4th – Friday 5th July 1991
Transmission Date
Tuesday 24th September 1991 at 9.00pm

Cast
Richard Richard – Rik Mayall
Edward Hitler – Adrian Edmondson
The Gasman – Mark Lambert
Mr Rottweiler – Brian Glover
Lolly – Gabi Valenti

BARB Ratings
5.6m (71st/3rd)

Daily Mirror Blurb

'It's some time since Rik Mayall and Adrian Edmondson first sprang on to our screens with the Young Ones, but there's no sign that they've matured in the years since then. This series sees them serving up the same brand of low-level schoolboy humour and it's a

treat. This week, there are problems with a neighbour and with the gas.'

Synopsis

Whilst playing a game of cards (well, cheating), Richie and Eddie are keeping warm with the blazing gas fire, and all the gas hobs roaring. So when the Gas Man arrives to read the meter, they panic, because they've been stealing next door's supply with a jerry-rigged hosepipe.

After their efforts to distract the Gas Man fail, they resort to violence, and seemingly kill him. But while plotting on how to dispose of the body, he comes to, and leaves, disoriented and having not read the meter.

Scared by this brush with authority, they attempt to disconnect their illegal supply, but instead anger their neighbour, Mr Rottweiler, who is hosting his lover Lolly. A change of plan, and they smash through the connecting wall, only to realise too late that they've miscalculated, and broken through into Rottweiler's bedroom. Richie keeps watch, while Eddie goes to remove the hosepipe – though he gets distracted by all the food in the fridge.

Belly full, Eddie yanks the hose free and causes a massive fire. In the mayhem, Richie and Eddie manage to escape home, and brick up the hole in the wall. Job done, feeling safe, Rottweiler smashes through the wall and lunges for them.

Guff

Bottom manages to pull off a good trick, and in doing so it makes itself a much better sitcom for it. On the one hand, *Bottom* is a cartoon. A big, garish, violent, over the top cartoon. On its own, that would work, but it's also small, intimate, featuring tiny people with tiny minds. Where a cartoon is brash and vibrant, *Bottom* is absolutely grotty. It's one of the last sitcoms to have grimy walls, beaten up furniture, and a squalor that has seemingly vanished from our screens.

And one of the best examples of this dichotomy of styles is *Gas*.

Gas starts small, and erupts into cartoon violence. It highlights the skills of its writers and stars, and is easily one of the best episodes of a sitcom I personally have ever enjoyed.

From the opening card game, to the arrival of the gas man, we see the smallness of the show. Here's two trapped idiots, wiling away their lives in a shitty flat, betting chores because they have nothing else to gamble. It's easy to see the Beckett influence on Rik & Ade, but there's loads of Hancock here too, and plenty of *Steptoe and Son* as well.

No matter how many times I've seen this episode, it's hard to watch it without being swept along by it all, but I tried my best, just to try and see some new things.

From the beginning then …

How's that for an establishing shot? The grime on that blazing fire, the laziness of the discarded matches and bottle of Newcastle Brown Ale. This is a set that looks lived in, but it's also exactly where Richie and Eddie would live. The oven, all four rings lit, caked in grease, with two missing knobs (do your own joke). The set in general does a lot of character work, from the grotty underpants drying on the line, to the pot of Ajax, so old and dirty that it's been there for years, unused.

It would be easy enough to get any old table and chuck a grubby cloth over it, but Bob Warans went and found just the right one. Beat up, run down, knackered. And just the tat in the background. A cheap photo of Elvis, the snowglobe, the Eiffel Tower, and a single, sad-looking mop leaning up against the organ.

Anyway, the Gas Man arrives.

My goodness but this sequence is fantastic. Rik and Ade's performances are amazing, as is Mark Lambert's. The still camera as Eddie creeps away and creeps back is beautifully executed by Ed Bye.

And the logic of having no gas is a master class in spinning out a comedy idea. The conclusion of drinking cold tea is a great pay off, and using leaves and not teabags just sells the grossness even more.

I also never noticed or appreciated the snow on the windowsill before. Or the icicles.

Of course it's winter. And snow is falling.

There's even a chilly breeze blowing outside, which is a lovely touch.

Moving on.

I know Eddie isn't Vyvyan …

... but I love that he shares his progenitor's inability to tell the time properly.

I sat down to watch this episode thinking that once the story leaves the flat, it loses something, but I think I'm wrong. The arrival of Brian Glover and Gabi Valenti really ups the ante, and turns the denouement into a nice little farce.

Let's take a moment to revel in the choice of expletives.

This is where restriction helps creativity. Not being able to swear properly on the BBC gives the show an interestingly arcane language palette. It's not bloody hell, or even blimey, it's Bloody Nora.

They're not shagging, or even doing it, they're Having It Off.

Even in the 90s no one said that.

Anyway, my Grandad had a camera just like Eddie's.

I used to be fascinated by those square, disposable flash bulbs.

Rottweiler's flat, in juxtaposition to theirs, is much more modern but still looks a little dirty and lived in. I like the wallpapered bedroom door.

Then we come to the bit that I thought might make me cringe – Richie perving over the sleeping couple.

It's gross, but it's notable that while Richie objectifies in this scene, the camera does not. We're not supposed to be on Richie's side in this moment. A lesser show would have given us Richie's POV, and may not even have had any comeuppance.

And what a comeuppance, with Rottweiler bursting through the wall. Seeing Brian Glover bearing down on you like that must be terrifying.

Gas was the fifth episode recorded, and was staged in Studio 1 (TC1) at BBC Television Centre.

Mark Lambert, who plays The Gasman, also appeared in *The Young Ones*, as the Bank Manager in *Summer Holiday*.

Brian Glover, the angry Mr Rottweiler, also appeared in *An American Werewolf In London*. He lives at number 2.

Richie punches the gas man 22 times, kicks him three times, and Eddie hits him with the frying pan 15 times, for fun. Richie then punches him twice more.

Amal's Kebab Shop is just across the road from the flat.

An extended cut from the script occurs after they have seemingly killed the gas man. In it, they bicker about what happens in the film Jack The Ripper, by way of working out a plan to dispose of the body. They conclude they should run off into the night, cackling with capes flying behind them. Richie then looks for some scissors. 'No. Richie, we can't prance around the whole of London in your Batman cape throwing bits of dead body everywhere.'

CONTEST

Written by Adrian Edmondson and Rik Mayall
Produced by Ed Bye and Paul Jackson
Directed by Ed Bye

Duration
29m12s

Recording Dates
Sunday 24th – Monday 25th June 1990
Transmission Date
Tuesday 1st October 1991 at 9.00pm

Cast
Richard Richard – Rik Mayall
Edward Hitler – Adrian Edmondson
Miss World Commentator – Peter Marshall
Miss China – Fiesta Mei-Ling
Documentary Voice Over – Patrick Lunt

BARB Ratings
6.2m (65th/1st)

Daily Mirror Blurb

'Tasteless? Juvenile? Of course it is but who would want Rik Mayall and Adrian Edmondson to be anything else? Keep the sickbag handy and enjoy the fun. Richie (Rik) considers the meaning of life, and finds that as far as he's concerned, there is none.

Synopsis

Forlorn, Richie rehearses his suicide, but it turns
out it's just a ruse to guilt-trip Eddie into buying
him a pint. When Eddie returns home, in a mood,
he fails to see what's going on, until he sees Richie
with his head in the oven.

He tuts.

Richie gives up, while Eddie vents his frustration
from a bad day at the dole office. Tensions
rise when Richie's attempt at a low-cost meal
backfire, and Eddie admits his benefits have been
suspended because he has too many savings.

£11.80.

And he's spent the majority of that on a vintage
pornographic magazine. So he settles down in
front of Miss World in order to cheer himself
up. Richie's having none of it, and demands they
watch something else. Tempers flare, and Richie
throws Eddie out of the flat.

Alone again, Richie turns on Miss World and
begins to masturbate – but Eddie catches him
when he returns to apologise. Now with the upper
hand, he settles back down to enjoy the show – and
reveals he's put a bet on the outcome. But it's a long
shot.

Richie breaks the television, and blows a fuse.
Whilst Eddie is scrabbling in the dark to fix it,

Richie falls out of the window, and when the lights come back on, Eddie discovers the fake suicide note.

But Richie returns, and they take stock of their lot in life. Their bet comes to nothing, and Eddie cheerfully admits he lied about the bet, and instead spent the money on a slap-up grill before he came home.

Richie punches Eddie in the face.

Guff

While *Contest* was the third episode of *Bottom* to air, it was actually the pilot, filmed a year before the full series (Rik and Ade went off to make a movie each in the interim). As such, there's quite a few differences in the set, and the haircuts are a bit different, but what's remarkable is just how in tune it is with what the show grew into.

Contest is a single scene, and it's testament to Rik & Ade's writing that their characters are firmly established from the start. The philosophy of the show is evident from the very first shot too. A glum looking Richie, staring out through a greasy, rain-soaked window, looking utterly depressed.

That shot is gorgeous. Ed Bye sets the tone in that single frame.

I'm not sure how many sitcoms have ever opened with their main character seemingly contemplating suicide (while later in the first episode their only friend tuts on seeing their head in the oven, and then encourages them to actually do it), but *Bottom* does.

The dig at the restrictive and uncaring savings cap on benefits is precisely aimed, with such a paltry sum triggering a freeze in Eddie's dole money. They can barely afford to eat actual food, and now have to live on £11.80 for at least two months. This is post-Thatcher Britain, and they're just expected to turn to the TV for comfort.

That this episode can sit bang in the middle of the series and not stand out like a sore thumb is also remarkable. As pilots go, this one is about as accomplished as they get.

Even the pilot set, underdressed by necessity and budget, is a work of wonder. The grot and grime are there. The dilapidation. The sheer bleakness of it. Even that forgotten, sad bit of tinsel is in the corner. It's the embodiment of a run-down Britain, abandoned and forgotten by ten plus years of Tory under-funding. And two of its many victims sit in the grime, in a flat almost constantly being rained upon, trying everything they can to not just give into the nihilism of it all.

The arcane language is there too, with some interesting choices of words – 'Some of the things they're doing would make your nose bleed.'

A notable difference in the pilot is how Eddie refers to Richie. He keeps calling him Richard.

One of the boxes above the cupboards where games will eventually live is a Spears Weaving Loom, either a leftover from the previous occupants, or more likely something Richie has to while away the boredom. Or maybe he uses it to fix clothes.

A favourite moment of mine in the episode is when Eddie has been chucked out, and Richie starts warming up for his onanism (written in the script simply as 'he starts getting sexy'). The whole bit is brilliantly timed, and topped perfectly with Richie's shush.

Also, this exchange:

'Sod off, you stupid fat git!'

'Don't try and wriggle out of it by being all grown up.'

I wonder how many televisions Ade has destroyed in his time.

A good pilot script will find a way to state the theme of the show (I think), and the opening moments of *Contest* do this really well. But it's nice when Richie and Eddie slump, and take stock:

'Don't be stupid, Richie. People like us aren't meant to win things.'

'What are we meant to do, then?'

'Look, you get born, keep your head down and then you die – if you're lucky!'

'Come on! There must be more to it than that!'

'Well, there's the telly.'

'It's no good, I think I've reached my bottom.'

Nuggets

Contest was the pilot episode, and was recorded in Studio 6 (TC6) at BBC Television Centre on 24th and 25th June 1990, nearly a full year before the rest of the series was recorded.

The script for the documentary audio (nice statistic) was read by Patrick Lunt from the book *British Social Attitudes: The 1985 Report*, edited by Roger Jowell and Sharon Witherspoon, and published by Gower Publishing Co. Specifically, it's from Chapter 7, *Measuring Individual Attitude Change* by Denise Lievesley and Jennifer Waterton.

Richie tells Eddie to hide the fags – even though neither of them seems to smoke.

Eddie says that the flat is Richie's Aunt Mabel's. While he never expressly states that she owns it – indeed, we know from later episodes that it belongs to Mr Harrison, who owns the shop below – it is later clarified in *Weapons Grade Y-Fronts*, that Aunt Mabel pays the rent.

Eddie reads *The Sporting Life* newspaper.

Unseen characters, Mrs Longbottom and Mrs Pugh work at the dole office.

Eddie hasn't had a steady job since 1978. He was a bunny girl, for ten minutes.

Amal's Kebab Shop is Ahmed's Tandoori Takeaway on the pilot set, across the road from the flat.

Eddie owes £11,645.66p in overdue rent.

They appear to be decorating the bathroom. The set for this pilot sees the stairs in a different configuration.

Unseen character Nasty Linda sends a shiver down Eddie's spine when he thinks about spending another night with her.

While Richie is in his going-away place, a boom microphone casts a shadow across his shirt. Wonder why they've got one of those in the flat?

They have a cup and saucer set just like one my Gran used to have. It's a JAJ set made by Pyrex.

Eddie seems to be building an Airfix kit of a Gloster Gladiator, but he's been doing it drunk, because it's all wrong.

Script Cuts/Deleted Scenes

During dinner, a moment was never filmed, in which Eddie realises that Richie has been banned from the butchers. Again. I need to know the story of why he keeps getting banned.

This moment as they watch Miss World was never filmed, but worth sharing in full:

RICHIE: That's what I'm missing from life.
EDDIE: What, a quick nasty?
RICHIE: No Eddie, love. The love of a good woman. An English rose. A Scottish heather. A Welsh … dragon.
EDDIE: A German sausage.
RICHIE: Yeah, an Irish … wolfhound.
EDDIE: A Chinese takeaway.
RICHIE: A Spanish … omelette – any of those'd do for me, except the Irish wolfhound obviously.

EDDIE: But all right with a German sausage then?
RICHIE: All right Eddie, let's skim over the details, it's only a metaphor. Give him an inch and he makes a porn movie. Tcch. (Sighs.) Why haven't I got a girlfriend? I wish I had a girlfriend – it'd be someone to listen to me. All I've got is you Eddie.
EDDIE: Careful.
RICHIE: I wonder what sort of great bird'd suit me.
(Bottom: The Scripts, page 70)

It's interesting to hear Richie talking about love more than sex here, and expressing his need to talk to someone who actually listens.

In the script, the TV just explodes, instead of Eddie kicking it.
Also in the script but not shot, when Richie is in immense pain, Eddie offers to fetch a Band Aid. Richie replies 'take your time Mother Teresa!'.

APOCALYPSE

Written by Adrian Edmondson and Rik Mayall
Produced and Directed by Ed Bye

Duration
28m59s

Recording Dates
Thursday 20th - Friday 21st June 1991
Transmission Date
Tuesday 8th October 1991 at 9.00pm

Cast
Richard Richard – Rik Mayall
Edward Hitler – Adrian Edmondson
Shooting Gallery Stallholder – Mark Arden
Brenda The Ballgazer – Liz Smith
Nurse – Helen Lederer
Sir Roger Cobham – Roger Brierley
Stuntman – Nick Gillard

BARB Ratings
6.5m (60th/1st)

Daily Mirror Blurb

'More smut and innuendo from rude boys Rik Mayall and Ade Edmondson in another episode of the life as-a-failure comedy. The terrible twosome come into some money, but

their windfall brings them more sorrow than joy. And Richie has a close encounter with the Grim Reaper.'

Richie and Eddie are preparing the flat, making it look even more impoverished, in order to con Richie's Auntie Olga into giving them some money. A call comes through, and Richie learns his aunt has died, leaving him £600 in her will.

Having hidden half of it in the cistern, he takes Eddie and the other half to the funfair. High on their newfound wealth, they damage a stall, and when he tries to pay for the damage, Richie realises his wallet has been stolen. Eddie offers double or nothing, but shoots the stallholder in the eye. They are chased by the fare-workers, and end up hiding in the fortune-teller's tent. She insists they pay for a reading, and predicts that Richie is about to die.

They head for the hospital, where Richie demands a check-up and is given a clean bill of health. Relieved, they head for the lift, and a man in a wheelchair falls to his death down the lift shaft.

Richie is now convinced his demise will be brought about by an accident.

He spends the next three days in a bunker of his own making, and insists Eddie checks all the food for poison. When Richie notices a sag in the ceiling, he demands that Eddie move his piano. But before he can do so, it crashes down through the ceiling and narrowly misses Richie.

Richie is now convinced that Eddie is the harbinger of his death, and throws him out of the flat.

Alone now, he goes to bed, but Death bursts in (it's Eddie on stilts), and strikes a bargain for Richie's life. The £300 quid in the cistern ought to cover it. Running off with his haul, Eddie trips and falls down the stairs, revealing his treachery. The stallholder barges in, to return the missing wallet, but takes the £300 as payment for his eye operation. Richie kindly offers him a free kick of Eddie's knackers, which he gratefully accepts.

I'll be honest, I never really enjoyed episode four of *Bottom* all that much. *Apocalypse* feels a little too expansive in scope and has some dodgy character attitudes in it, but it does have its moments to be sure.

In the opening scene, where they set up the flat to bilk Richie's Auntie Olga (not Mabel, who owns the flat), I enjoyed the idea that they hid all the food in the cistern, that the dead fish is called Elvis, and that Richie mentions the Poll Tax.

It's also interesting that Richie seems to have grown up with money – his aunt having servants and all. There's a story in his downfall that's never been told. Maybe it involved an oven ready chicken.

At the fairground, we meet Mark Arden, doing a good turn as a menacing stall owner. On my DVD Richie's racist G-word epithet has been re-dubbed as Yobbos, which is odd considering the chapter title on the menu still uses that G word. This was a change made for the broadcast repeat.

There's a marvellous shot as Eddie takes his double or quits aim. I love how moments like this find their way into studio sitcoms.

I also love the set design on the fairground itself.

Liz Smith is excellent as Brenda, and Richie's penchant for newsreaders pops up again, this time with Julia Somerville.

In the hospital, we meet a nurse played by Helen Lederer. Is Helen one of the few actors to play different roles in the show?

There's a nice bit of set dressing here. On the wall at the reception desk there's a sign that reads 'Please note: do <u>not</u> leave flowers for families at reception! They must be taken to <u>wards</u>. Thankyou.' I've spent enough of my life in hospitals to recognise these hand-written passive aggressive notes stuck up everywhere. You don't often, if ever, see them on as dressing on TV studio sets.

Richie invokes the Falklands, lying that he served, which along with the Poll Tax reference firmly roots the show in the early 90s. It's interesting that one of these things represents Thatcher's supposed zenith, while the other was a large factor in her downfall. Not to get too philosophical, but Richie is the embodiment of that generation's mentality, wanting to invoke the spirit of the Blitz, even though he never experienced it, and his

Falklands appropriation is another aspect of that. His false patriotism belies his love for a country that couldn't care less about him. And so he overcompensates, and shows massive entitlement whenever he meets authority, such as here, barging past the queue, and demanding time with the doctor. It's the same thing he does in *'S Up*, and it's so well observed that it rings ridiculously true even now. *Bottom* was calling out Boomers seemingly long before anyone else.

It's worth taking a moment to explore Eddie's logic, wherein he mixes up Sean Connery with Michael Caine. He seems to be conflating the film *Zulu* with the film *The Man Who Would Be King*. It's a wonderful little delve into his mind, and gives us the still brilliant 'they would have won if they'd kept their eyes shut'.

Richie likes resorting to prayer, for a man who seems otherwise completely Godless.

Then the piano falls through the ceiling. Apparently the bed fall in *The Young Ones* was done live (Lenny Henry remembers seeing it, and the reaction it got). I wonder if they did the same here. It's slightly diluted by having a cut, so maybe something went awry.

Nuggets

Apocalypse was the third episode recorded, and was staged in Studio 8 (TC8) at BBC Television Centre.

The opening scene of this episode was filmed a

week later, during the audience recording for *'S Up*. This may have been a remount to fix a problem with the scene, or more likely, they ran out of time on the pre-record day, and the Living Room set needed to be struck to make way for the sets used for the Audience Recording day.

Twenty supporting artists were employed for the more expansive scenes at the fair and in the hospital. The old man who falls down the lift shaft was played by Ray Chaney.

Mark Arden was a staple of the alternative comedy scene, alongside Stephen Frost as *The Oblivion Boys*. He shows up a number of times in *The Young Ones*.

Liz Smith plays the wonderfully named Brenda The Ballgazer, while Helen Lederer, as the nurse, makes cameos in *The Young Ones*, *Happy Families*, and *Filthy, Rich And Catflap*.

Nick Gillard performed the stunts in this episode. He later went on to co-ordinate all of the fight sequences in the *Star Wars* prequel trilogy. Moreover, he was a stunt performer on the original trilogy, and in the Indiana Jones movies.

The fish is called Elvis.

As Eddie guards all the food back at the flat, there's the first breaking of the fourth wall in the series, when he looks to camera knowingly.

Richie and Eddie have been saving a box of liqueur chocolates for their anniversary – what anniversary?

Auntie Olga's phone number is Little Piddle 338.

Richie has an annual membership to Barbarella's Fitness Centre.

Unseen character Mrs Tinkerbottom works for Auntie Olga. Richie saw her when he was four with the chauffeur and a bucket of fish.

The stall in the fare is called Hey Big Shot!

Richie has a gorgeous blue bakelite rotary dial telephone beside his bed, as well as an ashtray.

There's also a large pile of board games in the corner, including *Cluedo*, *Buccaneer*, *Monopoly*, and *Trivial Pursuit*.

There are a load of paint cans on the landing outside of Richie's bedroom. This suggests they are being very lazy about re-decorating.

Script Cuts/Deleted Scenes

There are only a few minor moments that were scripted but never made it to the screen:

- Richie sets up reception being on the top floor and the lift being out of order in dialogue, but this is done simply with a sign on the lift on screen.
- A small, obvious once you know it's

there, cut after Eddie explains how Richie injured himself in the Falklands, to excise the line 'really nasty gash, kept the plaster on for days'.

- A moment when Richie is fearful he may be blown up by a fleeing terrorist.
- An extra round of I, Spy with 'Death'.

'S UP

Written by Adrian Edmondson and Rik Mayall
Produced and Directed by Ed Bye

Duration
29m24s

Recording Dates
Thursday 27th – Friday 28th June 1991
Transmission Date
Tuesday 15th October 1991 at 9.00pm

Cast
Richard Richard – Rik Mayall
Edward Hitler – Adrian Edmondson
Mr Harrison – Roger Sloman
Mr Cooper – Michael Redfern
Doctor – John Wells
Old Lady – Evie Garratt
Old Lady's Son – Tony Caron
Shop Looters – Clive Thompson and Ben Losh

BARB Ratings
6.4m (66th/2nd)

Radio Times Blurb

'A black comedy series written by and starring former "Young Ones" Adrian Edmondson and Rik Mayall.

The backbone of Britain lies in its corner shops. But Britain's vertebrae are close to total collapse.'

Synopsis

Bored on a Sunday, Richie is restless, and annoying Eddie, who is trying to watch pornographic videos. When he finally gets Richie to calm down, they realise that they've been swizzed, and the videos are not at all dirty.

Their landlord, Mr Harrison bursts in, and demands that they go downstairs and look after his shop, because he has to go to his mother's funeral in Penge. The power goes to Richie's head, and he wears a white shopkeeper's coat, and makes Eddie wear his jacket backwards in lieu of a brown one. As the morning goes on, Richie finds his customer service skills wanting, and has his head bashed on the counter. He also threatens an old woman who has caught him talking to himself.

Eddie is bored, and concocts a plan whereby they can leave the shop unattended, by the cunning use of a bell, and instead go up on the roof and watch the cricket.

As petty revenge for a number of slights, Richie sets a trap for Eddie, but times it wrong, and leaves them stranded on the roof. Eddie shimmies down the drainpipe to stop the shop being looted. When he returns to the roof, the door slams shut once more, and the heavens open. Richie, incensed, punches Eddie off the roof.

I remember watching *Bottom's Up* when it first aired, and being surprised by a few things. It's essentially a bottle episode, albeit set in a few different places, but it's mostly just Richie and Eddie. It has an odd pace to it, an unusual structure, and a few revelations that changed the feel of the show for me.

But let's start with Eddie and his VHS tapes.

His line about spending an hour choosing his films rings so true with anyone who spent any time wandering around video shops in the 80s and 90s (or trawling streaming platforms now). This was probably early enough that the tapes were just in the newsagents, or in an independently owned shop above a record shop or something. Not really ready for chains just then.

Eddie and Richie also only really ever mention their mothers. This is interesting. They rarely talk about their fathers. That's a deliberate character choice, and informs them as people I think.

When Mr Harrison, the landlord arrives, we meet the always excellent Roger Sloman. This is the first thing that jarred with me, because before now, we have been told the flat belongs to Richie's Aunt. No matter, it's later clarified that she merely pays the rent, so Eddie saying it's her house is technically correct.

I think one of the reasons this episode feels a little different than the ones before it is because this is the first time we're seeing the flat during daylight, and it's not raining. Maybe.

Then we head down to the shop.

Another eye-opening moment upon first viewing. We never knew before now that the stairs down from the flat lead out into the shop itself. That's awkward. The boys have to enter and exit their home via the shop.

And the shop set itself is fantastic, with lots of attention to detail, and some now defunct brands, including Biarritz chocolates. And you can also get your photo-copying done here.

The timing of the hatch gag crushing Eddie's crisps is fantastic, and wasn't in the original script, suggesting they worked it out on the set in rehearsal.

It's interesting that when Richie and Eddie run back upstairs, we miss a flight entirely, and cut straight to the top floor. I say 'interesting'.

Also worth noting is the sign at the foot of the stairs up to the flat – 'This Is Not A Toilet'.

I wonder how often people have pissed on them.

Up on the roof, and another lovely set. A nice touch is the added reverb on the audio, giving a much bigger scale to the piece. Ade and Rik spoke about this on the Film Buffs show. Adrian began by saying 'we very much like to create our own world. We do in television as much as on tour ... there was a scene in *The Young Ones*, very early on, where we walk down the High Street because they're crossing to a pub, and it always troubled me that these kind of slightly larger than life characters suddenly were in the modern world, with proper motor cars and ordinary people in headscarves in the background - and we suddenly looked like crap pantomime people. So we've always since then been very kind of specific about creating worlds for the characters to live in where they don't appear ridiculous,

where there's enough level of belief that you can then do your own jokes.' Rik adds 'absolutely everything is under our control, even when we had rooftop scenes in *Bottom* – it's a pretend rooftop with a pretend backdrop, just so you might not have something real bleeding into the picture.'

Eddie eats a pickled onion sandwich exactly like the ones I used to make as a four year old. Bread. Single onion in the middle. All washed down with a deep swig of the vinegar from the jar.

The old woman saying 'bust him in the goolies' is fab.

Finally, we see Richie's Boomer mentality here again, appropriating history once more in an effort to feel bigger, and when he is given some actual, real authority, it goes straight to his head. He even immediately implements a class structure. Major's government would soon be echoing his sentiments and romanticising the British corner shop as a cornerstone of its antediluvian Back The Basics campaign. Indeed, much of Richie's dialogue in this episode would have been right at home in a Tory conference speech.

S' Up was the fourth episode recorded, and was staged in Studio 8 (TC8) at BBC Television Centre.

Roger Sloman is a long-time collaborator with Rik Mayall, beginning with *A Kick Up The Eighties*, and *The Young Ones*. Michael Redfern also made appearances in *The Young Ones* (*Interesting*), The Dangerous Brothers, and *Filthy Rich And Catflap*.

Mr Harrison is described beautifully in the script thus: 'Mr Harrison bursts in. Mr Harrison is always in a bad mood.'

On the door that presumably leads up to the flat, there hangs a sign that reads 'This Is Not A Toilet'. This is mentioned in the script.

The whole business with the counter top and hatch is not in the original script, and was probably found during rehearsals.

Richie alludes to Rachman regards Mr Harrison. Peter Rachman was a notorious slum landlord in the 1950s and 60s. He also owned the mews house from the Profumo scandal, and briefly dated Christine Keeler.

When the kids sing *Happy Birthday* in *The Furry Honeypot Adventures*, they are recorded for music rights reasons as The Bear Bums.

Between takes in the shop, Rik notices a review for *The New Statesman* in the prop newspaper, *The*

Sport. That series was enjoying a repeat run on ITV during June of 1991. This can be seen in the *Fluff* section on the Region 2 DVD.

The entire top shelf all around the shop is jammed full of toilet paper.

The front page headline on the *Sunday Sport* that Eddie reads in the shop is 'Voodoo Yoga Made Me A 17st Nympho'.

Unseen character Ethel Cardew is Richie's only ever girlfriend, and Eddie shagged her.

You can get your photocopying done in the shop, only 15p each.

Unseen character Tubbs Lardy broke the fire escape.

Here's the second time they break the fourth wall, when Richie says it doesn't do to heckle with Eddie.

Script Cuts/Deleted Scenes

There's a few lines cut either for time or pacing, when the Doctor points out the sign says 18 or over, and Richie smacks Eddie about the head a few times.

ACCIDENT

Written by Adrian Edmondson and Rik Mayall
Produced and Directed by Ed Bye

Duration
29m20s

Recording Dates
Friday 12th July 1991
Transmission Date
Tuesday 29th October 1991 at 9.00pm

Cast
Richard Richard – Rik Mayall
Edward Hitler – Adrian Edmondson
Spudgun – Steven O'Donnell
Hedgehog – Christopher Ryan
Boris – Mark Williams
Willy – David Lloyd
Open University Announcer – Rupert Bates

BARB Ratings
6.1m (79th/2nd)

Radio Times Blurb

*'Last in the black comedy series written by
and starring former "Young Ones"*

Adrian Edmondson, Rik Mayall

Synopsis

Eddie is nursing a hangover, so it's no good that Richie is overly-excited about his birthday. Eddie in unimpressed by Richie's obviously faked birthday cards, much to the latter's chagrin. To appease him, Eddie hands over a birthday present – a piece of paper that reads 'Madam Swish, 3.30'.

Believing this to be a booking for an escort, Richie is disappointed to learn it's actually a sure-fire tip on a horse race. And all he has to do is give Eddie the twenty quid to put the bet on at 10/1.

The horse wins, Eddie returns drunk and loaded, and tricks Richie into accepting £2 of winnings. But in doing so, he causes an accident, and breaks Richie's leg. They get back from the hospital just in time for the party the start. Only two guests turn up – Spudgun and Hedgehog, both of Eddie's friends. Hiding his misery at the rejection, Richie musters them to play Sardines, which Eddie uses as a ruse to wheel him into a cupboard and leave him there while they all spend the night watching telly.

Richie finally wheels himself from the cupboard, but falls down the stairs and breaks his other leg.

While Richie is at the hospital, Eddie invites everyone from the pub over to party after last orders, and when Richie returns, Eddie convinces him they are all his friends. Excited once more, Richie becomes obnoxious. He insults Boris, who suggests they all give Richie the bumps.

Bottom is at its most pure, and often its most brilliant, when it's just Richie and Eddie stuck in one another's claustrophobic company. It's testament to the writing though that the show can expand and grow as needed, and the way this is best achieved can be seen in the final episode of the first series, *Accident*.

Even though the action all takes place in the flat, mainly the kitchen and living room, this show seems a lot bigger than the other bottle episodes.

This is done in a rather elegant way. *Accident* opens with an extended scene featuring just Richie and Eddie, before Spudgun and Hedgehog join them, and finally the flat is jammed full of people. It's a progression that seems natural and works well.

Accident is a great episode, but not one that sticks out. I wonder if this is because of the more expansive nature of it.

I know I keep talking about the grottiness and bleakness of the set, but it always has something new to discover. Look at the light switch on the wall when Richie enters.

The whole sequence with the birthday cards is quintessential *Bottom*. Richie being his usual obnoxious self in an effort to disguise his massive shortcomings and loneliness, with Eddie pushing him as far as he dares. Ade's exasperation is pitched perfectly, and Rik's exuberance equally so. The line 'I was going out with my real friends' gets a laugh, but it cuts right to the bone of Eddie's relationship with Richie.

The whole Madame Swish run is brilliant. Characters talking at cross purposes is always a good comedy conceit, and here it works so well. It's the escalation that does it. And the way Ade rides the laugh after the red hot tip line is a masterclass. Likewise, Rik rides an equally big laugh when he drinks the 'sherry' later.

Bottom manages to seem timeless. A lot of that is due to the arcane language, and the already massively outdated set dressings. So it's really odd to see some proper 1990s cars when we ride atop the ambulance.

I think singing himself Happy Birthday is one of the most honest moments of self-reflection we ever see from Richie, and it's a little heart-wrenching, even though not enough to excuse his vile behaviour. Rik's performance again is spot on.

Let's take a moment to acknowledge just how good Christopher Ryan is. He gets a bad rap for Mike in *The Young Ones*, but he IS Mike, and he's great as Mike. I don't think Pete Richardson would have been good in that role. And here, as Hedgehog, Ryan is brilliant. He's got some of the best lines in the whole show. Steven O'Donnell is marvellous as Spudgun too.

Also, take a look at Mark Williams' outfit. That greasy hair. The far too tight top, and far too short trousers. The red socks.

A final note to say that as written on the page, the

first scene reads rather flat, but as performed, it's brilliant. So much of the nuance and reaction is unscripted, and it is testament to Rik and Ade that these characters exist in their world so clearly that there's no need to write it down.

Nuggets

Accident was the final episode of the first series to be shot. It was staged in Studio 1 (TC1) at BBC Television Centre.

This episode aired a week later than it should have ordinarily, because it was pre-empted by the coverage of The Man Booker Prize For Fiction (won by The Famished Road by Ben Okri).

Bottom was replaced in the schedules after this week by *Quantum Leap*.

This episode did not have a pre-record day in the studio. Instead, anything complicated that would have held up the evening's recording in front of the live audience was shot in the morning.

The moment when Richie breaks his leg was used for the clip during the *British Comedy Award* nominations in 1992, when *Bottom* was nominated for Best New TV Comedy. It won, beating *Terry And Julian* and *2point4 Children*. Ed Bye accepted the award.

The shot from atop the ambulance as it speeds along was originally filmed for an instalment of *Panorama*, the BBC's flagship current affairs show.

It was shot along the High Street in Aldershot. This is the only time we see the real outdoors in *Bottom*, everything else is always a set.

We get the final breaking of the fourth wall of the first series, when Eddie makes a face to camera.

Christopher Ryan of course played Mike in *The Young Ones* and Mell in *Happy Families*, but he was also a member of the cast (Lucky) in *Waiting For Godot* at the time this episode aired. He later appeared in the *Speaking In Tongues* episode of *The New Statesman*.

The music playing at the party is The More I See You by Chris Montez. Richie expressly mentions this in the script but it was cut for time. 'If he's not sexy, I'm a ridiculous old prat!'.

Richie owns a pair of girl-bait underpants, much like Rick in *The Young Ones*.

Richie mentions Norris McWhirter, of *Record Breakers* fame, who also tried to sue *Spitting Image* for using a subliminal image of him pasted into a pornographic scene. He lost the case, with the Judge noting that it would be impossible to see it at normal speed. It was only discovered when McWhirter's nephew was moving frame-by-frame through his off-air VHS recording. The sketch in which the contested image appears also featured lots of images from *The Sun's* Page Three.

Board games on the shelves in the background

include *Cluedo*, *Buccanneer*, and *Orient Express*.

Richie pulling a pube from his mouth was unscripted. It gets a huge laugh from the audience, and causes everyone in the scene to burst into giggles. This can be seen in *Fluff*, and the corpsing is hidden with a cut to Spudgun reacting.

For some reason there's a small Christmas tree sitting on top of the organ. Maybe Richie has decorated the flat for his birthday.

Unseen character Ethel Cardew is mentioned again. This time we learn Richie got caught aboard the HMS Ark Royal in an effort to impress Ethel, but she got off with the arresting officer.

Eddie's nickname is Chopper.

There are more paint cans stashed on a shelf above the stairs down to the shop.

Script Cuts/Deleted Scenes

A whole run from the original script is omitted, in which Richie and Eddie prepare for the party, during which Richie chooses a record, asks Eddie to fetch two bags of nuts, admits he tried to sneak into a ballet school two weeks ago, and conflates a spoonerism with a metaphor.

DIGGER

Written by Adrian Edmondson and Rik Mayall
Produced and Directed by Ed Bye

Duration
29m13s

Recording Dates
Thursday 16th – Friday 17th July 1992
Transmission Dates
Thursday 1st October 1992 at 9.00pm

Cast
Richie – Rik Mayall
Eddie – Adrian Edmondson
Mrs Lineker – Lisa Maxwell
Mrs Gascoigne – Kelly Hunter
Natasha – Helen Lederer

BARB Ratings
5.1m (79th/2nd)

Daily Mirror Blurb

'Rik Mayall and Adrian Edmondson remain
triumphantly at the bottom of the heap in a
new run of the comedy series. Belly-aching is
the nearest geographically correct, while still
decent, description of the laughs it provides.
Sex, or the lack of it, remains a problem, and

now the two losers enlist the aid of modern technology.'

Synopsis

Richie and Eddie have signed up at a dating agency, and in spite of their embarrassing videos, they've been matched. Richie, who lied about being a Knight of the Realm, has been paired with the Third Vicountess of Moldavia. Eddie, on the other hand, has matched with Sarah Ferguson, and he leaves, insulted.

To pay for the posh grub for his date, Richie sells a kidney, and bribes Eddie to masquerade as his butler. Eddie is lecherous to the Viscount, and receives a beating from his master. After dinner, the Viscountess makes a proposal of marriage, and Richie tests his luck, asking if she believes in sex before marriage.

She does.

Richie heads to the bedroom to get ready, while Eddie tries to get to the bottom of things. He gets her to admit that she's marrying for the money, and convinces her that he too has a bob or two. She agrees that he can be her back-up.

When she finally gets into Richie's bed, naked, Richie's body betrays him, and he suffers a heart attack.

In the ambulance, Eddie reports the subterfuge, and concludes that it wasn't a heart attack, it was the result of the dodgy kidney surgery, before accidentally revealing that he and the Viscountess had sex while they waited for the ambulance. Richie electrocutes Eddie with the defibrillator paddles.

Reviews

'There's nothing quite like a good old fashioned laugh. And there's nothing quite like Bottom to provide it. This Steptoe and Son with added physical violence, stars Rik Mayall as Richard and Adrian Edmondson as Eddie. Richie spends his time dreaming of escape from his grimy life in his grimy flat and of trapping a woman (grimy or otherwise). Hence the importance of his date with a Moldavian aristocrat he finds at Lilly Linneker's Love Bureau. Richie and the Countess are just beginning to enjoy their mashed potato and caviar when Richie realises - thanks to his "down to earth" flatmate, Eddie - that caviar is just "expensive fish poo". And it's downhill from there. When the Young Ones first came on the scene, it broke new ground in the same way as Monty Python did before it. Rik Mayall and Adrian Edmondson are still, to some extent, living in the reflected glory of the show which gave them fame. But although there is a limit to the amusement value of one person repeatedly beating up another, so far I can still get a good laugh.'

(MARK SMITH, ABERDEEN EVENING EXPRESS, 2ND OCTOBER 1992)

'Bottom, the creation of alternative comics Rik Mayall and Adrian Edmondson, could not be more appropriately named. For in comedy terms, you can't sink much lower than this. Mayall and Edmondson play a pair of repulsive flat-mates obsessed with bodily parts, bodily functions and inflicting grievous bodily harm on each other. When Rik brains Adrian with a brolly, he may have left his pal needing treatment, but he was never going to have me in stitches. Ninety percent of the humour in the first of a new series relied on the use of the double meaning. And so, for example, when a woman at the dating agency asks Rick, "Shall we have a look at yours then?" – she means his video but he drops his trousers. Jokes like this require a minimum of imagination.'

(GERRY CORNER, LIVERPOOL ECHO, 5TH OCTOBER 1992)

Guff

It was inevitable that Richie and Eddie would end up in a love bureau at some stage, and it's a good way to reintroduce the characters to the audience at the start of a new series. These two live in a very white, very male world, so it's nice that we get to meet Lily for an extended time – and she's played quite brilliantly by the always excellent Lisa Maxwell.

There's a rare mention of a contemporaneous

celebrity, and it's a rather cheap jibe at Sarah Ferguson.

The flat seems to have become even more grubby since we last saw it, with even more grime and slime everywhere, and lots of rubbish gathered into nooks and crannies.

Helen Lederer gives a well-pitched, understated performance too, remaining a centre of calm in this cartoon world. The way she goes about her business all the while is worth focusing on when your eye may otherwise be on Richie or Eddie. And she so very nearly corpses when Eddie puts his leg up on the chair. The flash of evil when she declares her true opinion about poor people is spot on with the bile. She gets an awful lot of mileage from a perhaps under-written character, and brings her to life. Even her reaction to Richie offering her arm isn't in the script.

I'm a little ambivalent about *Digger*. On the one hand it's full of great performances (Rik reading the sex manual is fantastic), and does the neat trick of giving Richie exactly what he wants, and then making him pay for it with a heavy, self-inflicted price. On the other hand, it resorts a little too often to double-entendres and does little to undermine the gold-digger trope (although Richie is just as guilty of this as Natasha).

That said, I can see why it was chosen as the series opener, because its story and the character dynamics are abundantly clear, and bring us back into the world of *Bottom* in a neat way that cleverly echoes *Smells*.

The Travel Show gave way for the new series of *Bottom*.

Digger was staged in Studio 1 (TC1) at BBC Television Centre, and the warm up was conducted by Andy Bull. It was the last episode of the second series to be recorded.

Other comedy on the same night included *As Time Goes By*, *Waiting For God*, and a repeat of *One Foot In The Grave* on BBC One, while Channel 4 had *My Two Dads* and *Rising Damp*.

Between series one and two, John Major's Conservative Party had won, somewhat unexpectedly, a General Election. It had a slim majority, which would eventually disappear, but dashed hopes of a Labour government, and cemented Tory rule for another five years.

Helen Lederer returns as a different character. Her full name is Lady Natasha Letitia Sarah Jane Wellesley Obstromsky Ponsonsky Smythe Smythe Smythe Smythe Smythe Oblomov Boblomov Dob, third Viscountess of Moldavia.

Richie claims to be the Duke Of Kidderminster.

In *Fluff*, from this episode (and others), Ade looks into camera and does an impression of Paul Nicholas from *Just Good Friends*, the hit sitcom written by John Sullivan. Also, between scenes Ade plays the organ for the audience.

The shot atop the ambulance is re-used from *Accident* – and was first filmed for an episode of *Panorama.*

This is the first episode that Richie does not have the opening line.

The dating agency is called Lily Lineker's Love Bureau.

Eddie breaks the fourth wall for the first time this series, when he reacts to hearing that Richie has quite a lot of nob in him. And a second time in the ambulance at the end.

The woman who comes to the door with a charity tin is called Mrs Gascoigne.

Continuing the football motif, one more role was filmed but ultimately cut, featuring Miss Beardsley, played by Nadia Sawalha, the love bureau's receptionist.

Eddie's tiny, impotent gong is simply a saucepan in the script.

As scripted, it just says 'Eddie reacts suitably' when he pants for breath and faints.

Richie owns a copy of *More Joy Of Sex.*

Unseen character Harry Belafonte, shouted her name at Eddie over her shoulder as she fled into the night.

Unseen character Harry 'I'll Do Anything For Half A Pint' Grundy still has their potato masher. It's stuck in his abdomen.

Script Cuts/Deleted Scenes

An entire opening scene was shot but not used. Much of the material was repurposed for *Bottom: Live* and series 3. It can be found on the DVD for series 2. It's a shame, not least because the waiting room set is marvellous, but also because it contains probably the best fart gag in the whole series.

CULTURE

Written by Adrian Edmondson and Rik Mayall
Produced And Directed by Ed Bye

Duration
29m10s

Recording Dates
Sunday 17th – Monday 18th May 1992
Transmission Date
Thursday 8th October 1992 at 9.00pm

Cast
Richie – Rik Mayall
Eddie – Adrian Edmondson

BARB Ratings
4.7m (87th/4th)

Daily Mirror Blurb

'Disgusting duo Richie and Eddie apply what brains they have to an awesome poser - how do they fill in time now the telly has been repossessed? The more cultured will be horrified to hear that they discover chess'

Synopsis
Eddie and Richie attempt to do the crossword, but resort to cheating, before an exasperated Eddie

demands to know why they repossessed the telly. Richie tells him he knows full well why – Eddie used the telly money to buy some magic beans. Eddie retorts that they got behind with the rental because Richie was using the money to get his penis enlarged.

It was a scam.

Consumed by boredom, they begin a night of games and sophisticated bonhomie, which consists of Chess and a home-made cocktail mixed from the meagre leftover contents of the cupboards. Eddie spends the whole night teaching Richie how to play chess, and when Richie still fails to grasp the rules, it descends into an epic brawl. So when Richie finally reveals that they didn't take the telly after all, he just hid it behind the fridge in an effort to encourage conversation, Eddie smashes the set over Richie's head.

Guff

Culture is quintessential *Bottom*, and easily one of its best episodes (custardy underpants aside). It channels Hancock and Steptoe with its own unique voice, and captures the suffocating monotony of life in a deft way. By dragging everything out into tortuous detail, and wandering down blind alleys, it sums up Richie and Eddie's life in one, explosively violent evening. I think that's why the custard pants thing sits uneasily with me, because it undercuts that oppressive ennui for the sake of a couple of throwaway gags.

The set up is aided by some great directorial choices, framing Richie and Eddie together on the small sofa, and adding to the claustrophobia. It sells the telly gag brilliantly too, by only cutting wider for the first time on the reveal. Also, Richie and Eddie taking delight in thinking they've cheated the crossword system speaks so well to their situation, as does Eddie's frustration and wanting to just put 'bollocks'.

The inane logic of the mechanics of Pin The Tail On The Donkey without the requisite constituent parts is marvellous, especially as the anger escalates the longer it goes on. Richie poking Eddie in the eye at this point is understated by their usual standards, and this is a good choice, because it makes the eruption of violence at the end even more explosive (and cathartic).

It's a nice nod to Wodehouse that Richie has so many rich aunts.

When Richie is channelling 'Noel Wilde', it's probably no accident that it morphs into Tony Hancock.

There's a nice moment, touching by *Bottom's* standards, when Eddie expresses affection for Richie. There must be something that keeps them together, other than necessity, and for Eddie, it's the entertainment value of living with someone he considers to be insane.

And so Eddie's rising anger, as Richie dissects the rules of chess in hilarious detail, sets up the finale so well that it's a massive tension release, and the reaction from the audience tells you just how successful it is.

Eddie and Richie both address the viewers from the fridge, before the reveal that the whole painful evening has been totally self-inflicted by Richie, just because he's lonely and wanted some meaningful company. The only thing that speaks louder than that to his character is when his best, and only, friend smashes the telly over his head.

Culture was staged in Studio 8 (TC8) of BBC Television Centre, and was the second episode of series 2 to be recorded. The warm up act was Pierre Hollins.

Hancock's Half Hour has an episode called *The Set That Failed*, in which Tony and Sid spend an evening without the television. It first aired in 1959 (when Rik and Ade were just toddlers), and doesn't appear to have been repeated until 1997. It's interesting to compare how this show and *Culture* set up the premise and where they diverge. Hancock immediately shows some repairmen trying to fix the set, while Richie and Eddie do a crossword as a nice misdirect from the big reveal – whyyyy did they take the telly away?. And let's take a moment to admire the set dressing for this shot, with a square of pristine table amidst the gross detritus of old crisps and dust.

Sid and Tony indulge in some culture, by way of a jigsaw and a conversation, with Tony sporting a smoking jacket that bears some similarity to Richie's. Both shows have characters attempting to watch the neighbour's TV with binoculars, but that's where the stories diverge. Tony and Sid wander into their neighbours to watch, while Eddie and Richie play some chess.

Eddie has the first line of the episode, a rarity.

The Euro '92 football sticker album on the coffee table most likely belongs to Eddie.

Unseen character Harold is an ironmonger. They ate his dog.

There's a string of Christmas lights still slung around the window.

Unseen character Great Aunty Dorothy left Richie a chess set in her will.

There's a tin of beans and a toilet roll inside the bread bin.

Eddie breaks the fourth wall again (five times), making faces to camera when claiming they don't have a chess set. Later, he also does his Esther Rantzen impression to camera.

The final chess board consists of five white playing pieces, an empty toilet roll with a face painted on it, a Scotch miniature, Mrs Plum, the yoghurt pot, a Spiderman plastic figure, an Airfix model of a skeleton, an ordinary 'greasy caff' pepper pot, a bottle of squeezy brown sauce, one of those ketchup containers shaped like a tomato, a pork pie with a flag stuck in it bearing the portrait of Sue Carpenter, a small cactus (with a paper crown), a small stuffed bird, a sausage, and sixteen slowly defrosting prawns.

There's also a McEwan's Lager ashtray on the table.

Unseen character Great Uncle Roderick died in an embarrassing drowning incident.

Eddie's reaction on learning Richie doesn't know the rules of chess is described in the script as 'Eddie does a Fluff Freeman'.

Eddie explains the rules of chess 124 times.

BURGLARY

Written by Adrian Edmondson and Rik Mayall
Produced and Directed by Ed Bye

Duration
27m58s

Recording Dates
Sunday 24th – Monday 25th May 1992
Transmission Date
Thursday 15th October 1992 at 9.00pm

Cast
Richie – Rik Mayall
Eddie – Adrian Edmondson
Mr Scrubbs – Paul Bradley
PC V. Jones – Jonathan Strait
Mr Wormwood – Rupert Bates
Jenkins - Sean Meo

BARB Ratings

4.9m (90th/4th)

Daily Mirror Blurb

'Eddie and Richie's dump of a flat is raided by a burglar who either must be very hard up or hasn't been watching the series.'

Synopsis

Richie is very angry as Eddie returns from fetching a fish supper, drunk instead, and without the food. When Eddie passes out, it's left to his old mate to drag him to bed, and after a crap day, Richie has nothing left to do but masturbate.

A sound from downstairs startles him, and he rouses Eddie to let him know they have burglars in the flat. Scared, they attempt to flee via the roof, but instead just fall down the stairs and crush the burglar.

They Sellotape him to a chair, and try their best to interrogate him. Richie finally calls the police, but hangs up halfway through when they find the burglar's bag of loot from an evening's robbing. Wild-eyed with greed, they poison the burglar with the pigeon pellets from the glass roof (where it's revealed a second burglar is still hiding).

When the police arrive, following up on the telephone call, the boys convince them nothing is awry. Still suspicious, the police leave, and Eddie reveals he has Sellotaped the burglar to the ceiling. The second burglar knocks them unconscious, and they awake to find the flat stripped clean, leaving them only their underwear, their balls resting on mousetraps, and an arousing note pinned to their knees. The traps snap shut.

Guff

The opening scene of *Burglary* nicely encapsulates Richie and Eddie's co-dependent relationship. It makes me wonder if perhaps Richie has a form of agoraphobia – he never seems to go out without company.

Richie and Eddie trying to look all hard, and great and cool in the extended run with the burglar is a great character study too. *Bottom* is often accused of just being slapstick and toilet humour, but there's so much more to it, especially in scenes like this. The wordplay, their idea of what's nefarious, their frames of reference, the twisted logic – it all paints them in more vivid colours. And nary a double-entendre to be heard.

And I like how their interaction with the taped up burglar and the tea echoes their shenanigans with the gas man. This episode doesn't quite hit the highs of *Gas*, but it's a damned good example of what *Bottom* is. The moment they find the silver, their demeanour changes, and it's all about grabbing a rare opportunity no matter what the cost. They can't obviously succeed, so ending up with their dicks in mousetraps is a brilliantly cartoonish way to bring them back down (by getting them up).

Nuggets

Burglary was shot in Studio 1 (TC1) of BBC Television Centre, and was the third episode of the series recorded. The warm up was conducted by Andy Bull.

The final scene was recorded the week before as part of the pre-record day for *Culture*.

The flat's address is 11 Mafeking Parade. This may be a reference to the Siege of Mafeking, a 217 day battle for the town in South Africa, which made a hero of Robert Baden-Powell. The son of the then-Prime Minister and Winston Churchill's aunt were trapped in the besieged town.

The two burglars are called Wormwood and Scrubbs. The policeman continues the footballing references by being named V Jones.

Eddie breaks the fourth wall again when he says he wishes he understood that, and wondering how this endeavour will end.

Stunts were performed by Tip Tipping (billed as Mr Kelly), who also did stunt work on Indiana Jones, *Batman*, *Never Say Never Again*, and *Aliens*.

The ladder to the roof has been confiscated by the police since some nurses moved in next door.

Neptune's Pantry, the fish n' chip emporium, is right next door to the Lamb And Flag pub.

PARADE

Written by Adrian Edmondson and Rik Mayall
Produced and Directed by Ed Bye

Duration
28m57s

Recording Dates
Thursday 2nd – Friday 3rd July 1992
Transmission Date
Thursday 22nd October 1992 at 9.00pm

Cast
Richie – Rik Mayall
Eddie – Adrian Edmondson
PC Cholmondley-Smythe – Robert McKewley
Chief Inspector Grobbelaar – Andy De La Tour
Spudgun – Steven O'Donnell
Dave Hedgehog – Christopher Ryan
Lil Potato – Patsy Rowlands
Veronica Head – Julia Sawalha
Mr N Stiles – Robert Llewellyn
Tight-mouthed Larry – Chris Langham
Ted Nugent – Robert Ashe
Ralph Maxwell – Robert Ashe
Mr Man – Roy Heather
Dick Head – Lee Cornes
Racing Commentary – Rory Bremner

Richie and Eddie, not for the first time, are "helping police with their enquiries". They're involved in an elaborate sting concerning a crooked bookie, a pretty barmaid and a Falkland's veteran with a tin leg.

Eddie and Richie earn some money by volunteering for a police line-up, but while on one of his self-righteous flows, Richie insults the Chief Inspector. Making haste with their wages, they head for the Lamb And Flag, only to find that the landlord, Dick Head, is away, leaving his niece Veronica in charge. They all pretend to be Health and Safety Inspectors, and get free drinks.

Richie flirts (badly) with Veronica, and claims loudly he was in the Falklands, which raises the suspicions of Mr Stiles, a veteran who lost a leg in the conflict. His wooden leg turns out to be worth a fortune. During all this, Tight-Mouthed Larry, the bookmaker, has staggered in, drunk as a skunk, and let slip that there's a dead cert at 100/1 in a race. The horse is called Sad Ken.

Richie and Eddie connive to steal the wooden leg, pawn it, and use the money to place a bet. They can then use the winnings to retrieve the leg and return it to Mr Stiles. The first part of the plan works, and Eddie heads out to the pawnbrokers and betting shop. Meanwhile, it's Richie's job to keep Mr Stiles distracted.

Sad Ken doesn't win.

It turns out that Dick Head, Larry, and Veronica were scamming everyone, and they've made thousands.

Needing money fast to retrieve the leg, Eddie and Richie mug someone in the toilets – that someone is the Chief Inspector. Later, he identifies them as his assailants at an identity parade, and instructs his constables to give them a damn good kicking.

Guff

Once again Richie gets to be self-righteous while being completely oblivious to his own shortcomings (he conspires in crime throughout this episode). His prejudices about criminals, on display here, as before in *Burglary*, and his need to appropriate the Falkland's war continue to skewer his generation's ideology. *Bottom* is a satire, hidden in a cartoon, its politics just as angry as *The Young Ones*, but targeted now at the people who enabled Thatcherism throughout a decade that bought those very same people to their knees. This is precisely encapsulated in Richie's immediate obsequious deference the moment he learns the man he's mocking as a criminal is in fact a Chief Inspector. It's perfect, the doffing of the cap to a system that will literally, by the end of the episode, give him a damn good kicking.

This is another story that neatly expands and builds the world around Richie and Eddie, adding layers of seediness with Tight-Mouthed Larry the dishonest bookmaker, Harry The Bastard, and petty cons as small victories against the system.

Richie's indifference to a soldier's suffering, and his knowledge of war being clearly gleaned from old World War 2 movies skewers him again. And I really enjoy Eddie's logic about the opposite of crying.

Richie fakes his patriotism, fakes his service, fakes his manliness, and berates anyone who doesn't do the same, all to counter his inadequacies – a tale that rings so true today that it gives me tinnitus. Now he would be a gammon-faced, alt-right, flag-hugging incel, screaming on Twitter in all caps about how it's just a bit of sun, or yelling for everyone to wear a jumper amidst a cost of living crisis. The deliberate timelessness of this world keeps it frighteningly relevant.

That all of this is wrapped up in a silly caper type plot is the essence of *Bottom*, and the amount of lines from *Parade* that have stuck with me through the years is remarkable. This episode is essential viewing even now – a solid half an hour that precisely dissects a socio-political ideology, with added nob gags.

Nuggets

Parade was staged in Studio 3 (TC3) at BBC Television Centre, and was the fourth show of the series to be recorded. The whole series was shot in two blocks, with three episodes shot in May, and three in July (possibly to accommodate Rik's stand up tour in June, or maybe to allow for more writing time). The warm up was Andy Bull.

More football references in the character names, including Nobby Stiles and Bruce Grobbelaar. Spudgun's mother is called Lil Potato.

Harry The Bastard may well be the same Harry The Bastard from *The Young Ones*. Here he runs a pawn brokers, while in the earlier series he was the unprincipled manager of the local Rumbelows.

Brian Croucher also appeared in *The Young Ones* and *Filthy Rich and Catflap*.

A policeman has the opening line.

Spudgun's mother gets to break the fourth wall at the end of the identity parade.

Nice line in the scene description of the script. 'Spudgun and Eddie look at Dave Hedgehog quizzically (and we don't mean like Bob Holness! Or do we? We're weird guys).

The toilets in the Lamb And Flag have been redecorated. Where they were purple before, they're now more of a claret colour. They have very quickly, and very comprehensively been defaced and dirtied.

Graffiti on the toilet doors reads 'Hello Wiggey'. Some on the wall says 'Robo Box' and 'Louis Is Bad'. Eddie is probably the one who scrawled 'QPR', and maybe even the one that says 'for a good spanking phone Edd'. An I.C.F tag is there too. The Inter City Firm was the name of a football hooligan firm associated with West Ham United throughout the 1970s, 80s, and early 90s. They were the focus of a Thames Television documentary called *Hooligan*, and the basis of Alan Clarke's 1988 film *The Firm*.

At the end during the identity parade, Spudgun is still staring, frozen with disbelief, at his betting slip.

HOLY

Written by Adrian Edmondson and Rik Mayall
Produced and Directed by Ed Bye

Duration
29m07s

Recording Dates
Thursday 9th – Friday 10th July 1992
Transmission Date
Thursday 29th October 1992 at 9.00pm

Cast
Richie – Rik Mayall
Eddie – Adrian Edmondson
Spudgun – Steven O'Donnell
Dave Hedgehog – Christopher Ryan
Mr Harrison – Roger Sloman
Valerie Bates – Tina Foley
Johnny Bates – Charlie Biddle

BARB Ratings
6.3m (73rd/2nd)

Daily Mirror Blurb

'Eddie and Richie's Christmas arrives rather early. For Richie it's a miserable time until he finds a baby on his doorstep. Suddenly his life

Synopsis

It's Christmas, and Richie is over-excited, even after a disappointing exchange of gifts. He begins to prepare their feast, and bans Eddie from watching the TV until the Queen comes on. Eddie contributes his own brandy butter substitute, and Richie accidentally chops off his own finger. Eddie crudely staples it back in place, before Spudgun and Hedgehog arrive. But the dinner is ruined, and they have to skip straight to the pudding.

The doorbell chimes, and Richie finds a baby on the step. He brings it in, and declares it all a Christmas miracle. All four vow to look after the child, before Mr Harrison comes in and reveals the child is his grandson. There's a real Christmas miracle for Richie and Eddie though, as the baby's mother settles down for his feed.

Guff

I actually fell off of the sofa laughing at the Virgin Mary scene when *Holy* was first broadcast. So it's fair to say I like this episode.

There's something annoyingly likeable when Richie is overly excited. His child-like fervour for Christmas is charming in many ways, and so is the honest selfishness of it (also child-like). And the unbending adhesion to Christmas traditions rings true too. So it's a nice contrast that Eddie is so grown-up, bored, and cynical about it all.

That's Christmas in a nutshell.

That said, Eddie did write a letter to Santa, and asked for a Star Bird, a Batman cape, and a ticket to the Bahamas. The Star Bird is a very 1970s toy, and a great choice for his character.

The honesty of Richie's mood turns when things aren't going well (God, I hate Christmas) points to the false bonhomie, giving both their characters a nice internal conflict with Crimbo, and adding to the all too real frayed tempers of the season.

If you watch this episode and don't quote 'fick urf you sad pathtic winker' throughout the rest of your life, you have more fortitude than me.

I think Richie's self-portrait is rather good actually, especially for fifteen minutes work.

Sprouts used to be disgusting. They're not wrong. But then in the mid-90s, Dutch scientist Hans van Doorn pinpointed the chemical that gave them the bitter taste (glucosinolate), and it has since been bred out of them.

Under-reaction is usually funny, but there's something even funnier about Eddie's 'oooh, that's a bit of a nasty nick'.

There's a rare visual effect, rather than a practical one, when Richie lights the Christmas pudding, but then it cuts to real flames.

'Jesus Christ! Who can that be?!' is a clever bit of foreshadowing when the doorbell rings, and there's a baby there.

Richie's reaction is rather touching, and the whole run of Eddie's fear that it will come between them is great. And then the careful plants are paid off to brilliant effect, huge laughs are ridden expertly, before naturally, the power goes straight to Richie's head, only for it to be yanked away from him once again.

I do wonder if this was meant to be an actual festive edition of the show. The excised and subsequently reinstated scenes for the longer running time support this assumption, but there's no record of why the plan was changed. On the Region 2 DVD as the title appears, it announces The Complete Episode, which also suggests it was always meant to be longer.

Nuggets

Holy was staged in Studio 3 (TC3) of BBC Television Centre, and was the fifth show of the series to be recorded. The warm up was conducted by Pierre Hollins.

The transmission running time for this episode meant that a full five minutes had to be cut – all of which was reinstated for the DVD release. The restored scenes include Eddie's letter to Santa, Richie's self-portrait, the Christmas tree and fire, Richie cooking, a discussion about getting someone in to breastfeed the baby, and Richie's commandments.

The only episode to end with no violence incurred on either Richie or Eddie. It's Christmas after all.

Eddie has stolen some roadwork gubbins, a hospital sign, a hairdresser's chair, and seems to be a Spider-Man fan, judging from the paraphernalia in his bedroom. He also has a roll of loo paper beside his bed. In fact, his whole room reminds me of Compo's house in *Last Of The Summer Wine*.

Richie's stocking is actually a pair of tights.

Eddie daubs football tags on the walls, and announces that 'Edie Is Grate'.

Eddie breaks the fourth wall with a sigh to camera when Richie unwraps a sprout, and again when he demonstrates perspective. Later, he makes a face to camera when he's let off peeling the spuds, and also when sighing that they could be drinking and watching television.

The phrase 'honi soit qui mal y pense' that Richie uses here, and in other episodes means 'shame on him who thinks evil of it', and is the motto of the Order of the Garter,

When Eddie is putting the fire out, there's a studio camera in shot on the left of frame. Eddie probably nicked it from somewhere.

'S OUT

Written by Adrian Edmondson and Rik Mayall
Produced and Directed by Ed Bye

Duration
28m12s

Recording Dates
Sunday 10th – Monday 11th May 1992

Transmission Date
Monday 10th April 1995 at 9.00pm

Cast
Richie – Rik Mayall
Eddie – Adrian Edmondson
Flasher (Mr Tent) – Rupert Bates

BARB Ratings
5.9m (2nd)

Daily Mirror Blurb

'Eddie and Richie are on a camping holiday, but little's changed. They have no food, no money - and little chance of survival.'

Synopsis
As a bet, Richie and Eddie have to spend a week camping on Wimbledon Common. They have come ill-prepared however - they have a tin-

opener but no actual tins. Eddie has bought some Hob-Nobs though, but refuses to share them. They fight, and the biscuits get soaked in a pond.

Eddie tries to hunt Wombles, while Richie goes fishing. He catches a minnow but it tastes disgusting. Fed up, Eddie drinks himself unconscious, before a flasher harasses them.

They retire to the tent for bed, but Richie cannot sleep because the fish is repeating on him. Scared by the sounds from outside, the owl hoots, and shadows, Richie winds up Eddie, who is convinced the Wombles are coming for them. He lights a fire to ward them off – but it's just the flasher, who has come back to wiggle in through the tent door. Eddie yanks the zip up, trapping the Flasher, who runs off in pain, taking the tent along with him.

Guff

Because of its long delay in broadcast, and only being available on VHS, *'S Out* always felt like a special treat somehow. It's the naughty one that got away.

I don't blame Ed Bye for showcasing the wonderful exterior set with a fancy crane shot at the beginning, and I love how even the idyllic outdoors looks grotty in the world of *Bottom*. It's real turf, real grass, and real foliage. Even the wrought iron Victorian lamp post looks real. And the shot of the Hobnobs sinking as Richie and Eddie collapse in the background is gorgeous. The whole set looks even better lit for night and in the rain.

Eddie reads his book in the tent upside down –

maybe his eyes really are the wrong way up.

The whole episode serves as a nice precursor to their stint on Hooligan's Island, and it's fun to see two idiots trying to survive in the wilderness, instead of trying to survive in the city.

This episode was delayed from its original broadcast, which should have been on 5th November 1992, because of a real-life murder on Wimbledon Common at the time. It finally aired as part of a repeat run of series two, but was included on the VHS tape release in 1993. It never appeared in contemporary listings, and so the decision to delay broadcast was not made at the last minute.

BBC Two replaced the episode with a repeat of *Blackadder Goes Forth's General Hospital*. Why not *Private Plane*?

When this series of *Bottom* ended, it gave way to the first series of *Absolutely Fabulous*. Adrian sings this show's theme *'This Wheel's On Fire'* in a duet with Julie Driscoll.

This is Rupert Bates second appearance of this series.

The only episode that does not end with a freeze-frame.

This is the first episode not to have a scene in the flat.

Eddie sighs to camera when asked 'who'd be

English?', and gives a wanker sign down the barrel of the lens when told they're great mates.

Eddie has a romantic interest who works in Sketchley's, the dry cleaners.

Unseen character Mad Ken Stalin bet them they couldn't live rough in the country for a week.

They have pitched their tent using a sign that reads 'Dogs Toilet'.

BOTTOM: LIVE

Written by Adrian Edmondson and Rik Mayall
Produced by Nicky Rose
Directed by Marcus Mortimer
Presented by Phil McIntyre

Duration
1h41m

Tour Dates (all 1993)
Wednesday 14 April – Rhyl New Pavilion
Thursday 15 April – Doncaster Dome
Friday 16 April – Hanley Victoria Hall
Saturday 17 April – Guildford Civic Hall
Monday 19 April – Brighton Dome
Tuesday 20 April – Kidderminster Glades Arena
Wednesday 21 April – Hull City Hall
Thursday 22 April – Bradford St Georges
Friday 23 April – Sunderland Empire
Saturday 24 April – Middlesbrough Town Hall
Monday 26 April – Glasgow Pavilion
Wednesday 28 April – Aberdeen Capitol
Thursday 29 April – Edinburgh Playhouse
Friday 30 April – York Barbican
Saturday 1 May – Newcastle City Hall
Monday 3 May – Bristol Hippodrome
Tuesday 4 May – Poole Arts Centre

Wednesday 5 – Thursday 6 May –
Wolverhampton Civic Hall
Saturday 8 May – Cambridge Corn Exchange
Sunday 9 May – Lincoln Ritz Theatre*
Monday 10 May – St Albans Arena
Tuesday 11 May – High Wycombe Swan Theatre
Thursday 13 May – Cardiff St Davids Hall
Sunday 16 May – Woking New Victoria Theatre
Tuesday 18 May – Sheffield City Hall
Wednesday 19 May – Liverpool Empire
Friday 21 May – Blackpool Opera House
Saturday 22 May – Scarborough Futurist Theatre
Sunday 23 May – Lincoln Ritz
Tuesday 25 May – Portsmouth Guild Hall
Wednesday 26 – Thursday 27 May
– Leeds Grand Theatre
Friday 28 May – Northampton Derngate
Saturday 29 May – Manchester Apollo
Monday 31 May – Birmingham Symphony Hall^
Wednesday 2 June – Nottingham Royal Centre
Friday 4 – Saturday 5* June – Oxford Apollo
Monday 7 June – Leicester De Montfort Hall
Wednesday 9 June – Southend Cliffs Pavilion
Friday 11 – Saturday 12 June –
Norwich Theatre Royal
Sunday 13 June – Brentwood Centre
Monday 14 June – Ipswich Regent
Tuesday 15 June – Reading Hexagon
Friday 18 – Saturday 19 June* –
Southampton Mayflower
Monday 21 June – Plymouth Pavilion

Tuesday 22 June – Margate Winter Gardens*
Thursday 24 June – Hanley Victoria Hall*
Saturday 26 June – Hammersmith Apollo*
Monday 5 July – Bristol Colston Hall*
Tuesday 6 July – Birmingham Symphony Hall*
* not listed on the official poster
^ a second date was added either the day before or day after this one

Recording Dates
**Friday 18th – Saturday 19th June 1993
at the Southampton Mayflower**

Original Release Dates
Monday 27th September 1993 (VHS)

VHS/DVD/Audio Cassette Back Matter

'Filmed during their sell-out 1993 nationwide tour which left over 250,000 fans in a state of complete delirium, this is Adrian Edmondson and Rik Mayall at their anarchic best.

For the first time unfettered by the restrictions of TV, 'Bottom Live' will transport you totally into the explosively insane world of two of society's most catastrophic no-hopers. This is Richie and Eddie as they were meant to be seen – a side of 'Bottom' that the BBC would never dare show.

Surviving on a diet of vitriol, mutually inflicted wounds, booze and rotting food, they belch, curse and smash their way through the boredom of life. The effects are, not surprisingly, quite disgusting!

Totally over-the-top, completely uncensored ... and bloody hilarious!'

Cast
Richie – Rik Mayall
Eddie – Adrian Edmondson

Synopsis

Richie and Eddie have spent the weekend locked in the lavs of the Lamb and Flag, so they really need some breakfast. The post arrives, bringing a letter and a parcel for Richie.

The letter is from the solicitors, and the package contains Monica, a blow-up sex doll that Richie has secretly ordered.

Eddie 'accidentally' opens the letter, and learns that Richie's uncle has died, leaving him £15,000 in the will. Eddie connives to claim the money himself, and even accepts a bribe to leave Richie alone in the flat.

Whilst seducing Monica, Richie superglues himself to her, and Eddie comes home intent on killing his flatmate for the inheritance money. After liberating Richie from the doll, Eddie attempts to poison him, but fails. That's when Richie reads the letter and learns that he is not inheriting the money, he is in fact in debt for £15,000, unbeknownst to Eddie.

Richie resigns himself to suicide, but not before

Eddie has tricked him into signing a marriage certificate. When he realises the truth, and this marriage mistake, he joins Richie in a suicide pact.

Reviews

'There'll Always Be Richie And Eddie

Bottom at the Wycombe Swan

For some, two fun-packed hours of X-rated slapstick is the ultimate nightmare. For others, it is a time to relax, laugh and marvel at the baseness of human nature. Fortunately, only the latter type were present at the Wycombe Swan to see Bottom. Richie and Eddie were on fine form with a feast of frolics, fungus, and farty jokes to see us through the evening. What can, at times, be a rather stagnant recipe on television was transformed into an amusing, lively, gripping (if that is the right word!) repartee for the stage show, starring Ade Edmondson and Rik Mayall. The pair romped around the remarkably accurate set, musing in typical Bottom fashion about the lack of available girlies, the scarcity of anything remotely edible, and the profound hate they seem to have for one another. The clever script was helped along by a host of amusing props; an inflatable doll called Monica, an electric toilet, and a packet of ancient Special K, though one or two additional characters would not have gone unappreciated. Tricky manoeuvres - namely beating the hell out of each other - were well handled in front of a live audience, with well-timed jerks and cries of agony accompanied by harrowingly realistic sound effects There was also a sprinkling of explosions and electrocutions thrown in for good measure. But the most amusing bit of all - whether genuine or not - was the moment when both Rik and Ade came out of character and ended up in stitches, taking the audience with them. All in all, the stage version worked well and received a good response from the audience. I think it is always a relief to know that, no matter how much of a sad case you are, there are always Richie and Eddie.'

(ZOE FISHER, RUISLIP AND NORTHWOOD GAZETTE, 2ND JUNE 1993)

'The Lowly Humour Of 'Bottom' Is A Real Gas

It began with a long, loud, fart and ended with an exploding toilet. What else could it be but 'Bottom' and the irrepressible Rik Mayall and Adrian Edmondson.

The hit TV series burst on to the Winter Gardens stage with usual mix of anal and banal banter which has these two masters of their art.

A brilliantly written script was supplemented by some side-splitting ad-libbing which had Edmondson claiming to have been born in Margate.

His relentless string of asides had Mayall in fits of laughter and demanding to return to the script before the pubs closed.

But Edmondson had his sidekick on the ropes and strung him along for some minutes before admitting he was waiting for Mayall to feed him the next line.

Mayall pulled himself together and delivered it, only to join the audience in fits of laughter again as Edmondson announced: "Aha! A line from the script!"

It was a great night's entertainment, made more so by fact that they seemed to enjoy it as much as the audience did.'

(HELEN MARSH, THANET TIMES, 29TH JUNE 1993)

'Bottom Really Was The Tops!

Crude, vulgar and revolting disgusting, is one way to describe the talented Rik Mayall and Ade Edmondson in their performance of Bottom at the Margate Winter Gardens, but the production was also downright hilarious.

After witnessing Richie and Eddie's uncouth antics in the popular BBC Two series Bottom, seeing the stage performance was an absolute must.

Not surprisingly the show's only Kent date was sell-out and was definitely not production for the narrow-minded or faint-hearted. Packed with toilet humour from the opening scene, the audience were constantly wiping away the tears of laughter ... An amazing performance from both actors, who struggled to keep to the script and had the Winter Gardens in hysterics.'

(MS, WHISTABLE TIMES AND HERNE BAY HERALD, 1ST JULY 1993)

'Young Ones Grow Up

Bottom, Symphony Hall

Tell people you are going to see a show called Bottom and they may think you are slightly mad.

And 'slightly mad' is a phrase Rik Mayall and Adrian Edmondson must be used to hearing after embarking on the TV series known as Bottom.

The award-winning show returned to the Symphony Hall at the weekend for a third time following two sell-out performances last month.

Fans just can't get enough of this popular duo who also brought to life the Young Ones, Filthy Rich and Catflap, and several Comic Strip Presents.

Rude noises remain a firm favourite and, along with the kind of slapstick comedy which makes your eyes water, the audience appreciated each and every carefully crafted line.

Almost like a grown up version of the Young Ones, the flat-sharing pair are Richard Richard, a rather pathetic sop desperate to find a girlfriend, and Edward Hitler, a sadistic beer swiller.

The stage version is as rude, outrageous, violent and bizarre as the screen shows. And Rik is still wearing those highly attractive elephant-sized Y-fronts.

For those who saw the BBC 2 run of shows,

(TC, SOLIHULL NEWS, 9TH JULY 1993)

Guff

I never had the chance to see any of the live *Bottom* shows, even though they often came to town. So I've only ever seen them as recorded, and *Bottom: Live* was a treat when I first got hold of it on VHS. It felt like such a different thing, seeing a sitcom performed on stage, because at the time I wasn't aware that this had been done before (Steptoe And Son had done it in Australia in 1977 for example). I get the selling point that it can be a lot ruder than the TV, and some of that material is marvellous, but one of the appeals of *Bottom* for me was always the arcane, dated 'obscene' language. But this first show strikes that balance very well.

The opening montage, reminding us that this is a live stage show, is nicely done, with the music from the auditorium playing as we watch some vox pops. I wonder where those people are now.

The flat set lends itself well to the stage, of course, being designed as it was for a studio audience, though it feels a little less grotty and claustrophobic here. And in case we're in any doubt, seeing the audience applaud upon Richie's entrance (oo er) reminds us that this is a stage show, not a sitcom episode. Thus, it's more theatrical, and rather less intimate. Rik and Ade are performing for the audience, not for the cameras, and so watching it on the small screen does feel a little off.

It's nicely filmed though, with good camera angles, and unobtrusive cutting between them.

There seems to be a bit cut after Richie ruins his underpants and before he finds the Special K.

Eddie banging his spoon is a great bit of business, as is Ade's reaction to his own banging.

Off all the live shows, this first one is the closest in tone to the sitcom, especially these opening moments at breakfast time. In fact, there's nothing too rude that wouldn't have been allowed on TV, and I think that's a deliberate choice – set the tone of the series, and then expand the boundaries.

There's a deft bit of misdirection by Ade, giving it one of his specials, building up while Rik switches the brick of cereal and grabs a mouthful of teeth. I can't even see when Ade loads his – but he may do it when we are looking at the audience.

Indeed, the stagecraft of all the slapstick is

flawless.

I like how the story gently unfolds throughout the morning, and we are just given a chance to spend some time with Richie and Eddie. When Eddie reads the letter from Shotgun, Bastard And Dribble, the sum of money he's prepared to betray his friend for is such a paltry amount. Fifteen grand.

I enjoy the breaks of character, scripted or otherwise (Ade admits that many of the goofs were real at least once, but repeated thereafter for the jape). They sell them so well that it's hard to tell which is real and which isn't.

I always wonder if Monica is actually supposed to burst at the end of act one, and if they ever managed to achieve the effect. The botched repair job with duct tape would suggest she is.

Just to drive home the timeless nature of the production design of *Bottom*, it's rather jarring to see the audience looking so very early-90s. Even the contemporary references (Graham Taylor) still fit, because there are so many other arcane references littered throughout (Rachman, for example).

There's something rather touching about Richie thanking Eddie for being his friend.

All in all, this first live show is an excellent instalment of *Bottom*, and sits nicely between the series. Indeed, I can easily see them reusing much of the material in future episodes had it not been filmed for prosperity.

Since writing of the second series unemployment had reached over three million once more, the Queen had her Annus Horribilis, Black Wednesday forced the Government to withdraw the Pound from the ERM, Charles and Diana separated, the recession continued, and the number of unfit homes is recorded as 1.3 million.

Rik told the Uxbridge Leader, in an interview about filming Rik Mayall Presents, but talking about this live show:

> *'There is a moment where Ade is supposed to kick me several times somewhere very painful. But at one performance instead of fractionally missing – which is what is supposed to happen – he actually made contact, very hard. I was writhing around in pain and he went to the front and said: "Is there a Doctor in the house?" Then he just laughed and said "Funny, wasn't it Doc?". I think most of the audience thought it must all have been part of the show, but all I can say is that it's a good job I've already got having kids out of the way.'*

(UXBRIDGE LEADER, 2ND JUNE 1993)

This first tour was simply called *Bottom* (or Bottom Live Tour '93), with the added information on the poster 'starring Rik Mayall and Adrian Edmondson in a full stage play based on the award winning

BBC2 TV series'. It became *Bottom: Live* for the VHS release.

The souvenir program included a never-seen-before script. There was also a souvenir t-shirt, featuring Richie and Eddie on the bench, which read 'who needs birds when you've got your mates'.

Before the tour began, Rik and Ade lay down on the bed with Paula Yates on *The Big Breakfast*, and joked that early sales for the Rhyl show were poor.

On Saturday 17th April 1993, Rik and Ade stopped by *Going Live!* for a chat with Sarah Greene and the kids. They did a sketch with Trevor And Simon, where both duos plugged their current tours. Ade has Rik in stitches with a bit he does on the fly with half a dozen telephones, and Rik mentions the show the night before in Hanley, describing it as great.

Unseen character Frank is eight inches long and three inches round, and feels the need to write this on toilet walls.

The headline on Eddie's newspaper is 'Hotel Bonk!'.

Unseen character Ethel Cardew has a return mention – Richie seems to be over their failed romance, and Eddie is now the one infatuated with her.

During their first big fight, with a high-pitched

voice, Eddie calls Richie Rik.

The Big One was a Channel 4 sitcom starring Sandi Toksvig and Mike McShane. It was written by Toksvig and Elly Brewer, and ran in the spring of 1992. Eddie makes negative reference to it, perhaps in response to an interview Sandi gave (I think on Anne and Nick), in which she said she loved Rik and Ade, but felt that *Bottom* was far too lavatorial.

Unseen character Gusty O'Windflap installed the pump under the sink so he could rehearse his adult variety act 'The Human Balloon'.

Eddie's Sunday Magazine has Noel Edmonds on the cover.

There's a pot of Nivea hand cream on the organ.

Eddie's middle name is Elizabeth.

One of the books on the bookshelf is The Brownie Annual from 1986.

Unseen character Dodgy Ken is a lawyer.

The painting which hides Richie's emergency fiver is Miss Wong by Vladimir Tretchikoff. It's a different print to the one on the window wall of the TV show's set, which is more vibrant and smaller. This was a popular picture to hang in homes in the 1970s.

There are some fun dual credits including tour

manager/chauffeur, stage manager/doll inflator, special effect/cider, deputy stage manager/ wardrobe, lighting designer/make-up, sound engineer/decisions, not a lot/very little, coach driver/merchandising, truck driver/running round for Pete.

On Triple J Radio in Australia, while promoting *Guest House Paradiso*, Ade revealed that the 'have a wank' heckle from this show was scripted and shouted by a roadie.

HOLE

Written by Adrian Edmondson and Rik Mayall
Produced by Jon Plowman
Directed by Bob Spiers

Duration
28m51s

Recording Dates
Tuesday 8th – Wednesday 9th November 1994

Transmission Date
Friday 6th January 1995 at 9.00pm

Cast
**Richie Richard – Rik Mayall
Eddie Hitler – Adrian Edmondson**

BARB Ratings
5.11m (3rd)

Daily Mirror Blurb

'Surprise return of the disgusting, but hilarious, series. Rik Mayall and Adrian Edmondson once again play Eddie and Richie, a sex-starved pair of morons determined to satisfy their foul appetites.'

Synopsis
Without realising the fair is closing, Richie and

Eddie climb onto the ferris wheel, and are stranded at the top when the power is turned off. Concern gives way to boredom, before Eddie reads in the paper that the wheel is scheduled for demolition in the morning.

They concoct a distress flare from a hip flask, but it falls back into the cabin and sets it alight. Richie stamps out the flames, the floor breaks, and he falls through. Trapped by his own fat waist, Eddie pulls him to safety by the hair. Incensed by this, Richie sits down heavily, breaking the support strut and putting them in even more peril.

They pray to God, who actually lends a hand, until they remember their atheism, God vanishes, and they appear to fall to their death.

Reviews

'It's been a long time coming, but thankfully Richie Rich and Eddie Hitler (no relation) are back with a brand new series of comic escapades. The mismatched and extremely violent pair made their debut back in 1991, hitting each other over the head with frying pans, poking each other in the eye, etc, and being generally revolting. On paper this doesn't sound like a barrel of fun, but in the hands of Rik Mayall and Adrian Edmondson, Bottom proves to be hilarious cartoon stuff, miles away from the safe sitcom world of The Upper Hand and So Haunt Me. In the opening episode, the gruesome twosome get

trapped on a fairground ride. Look out for the hilarious closing titles, set to the jazzy music of the Bum Notes.'

(ABERDEEN EVENING EXPRESS, 31ST DECEMBER 1994)

Guff

When *Hole* first aired, I forgot it was on, and remembered at exactly 9pm. So I rushed down to watch and record it, missing the first minute or so. Thus, for a long time, I never knew how this episode began.

And what a perfect sitcom idea this story is, and more importantly, it's a brilliant *Bottom* story. A simple, clear premise, that escalates the stakes, but still feels small, and intimate. It's a fun, interesting spin on the stuck in the lift trope.

It begins with a great set of establishing shots, showing off another audacious studio set, and manages to make the fair seem old and dated. Wonder if this is the same travelling fare from *Apocalypse* – and that's another reason they've been stranded atop the wheel.

Beginning with Richie and Eddie discussing how they've had a nice evening for once is great writing, and a good setup to the ride breaking down. Not often we see them enjoying themselves, in their own unique way. And Eddie looks good in a skirt.

Then the good mood gives way to an argument that just keeps getting more tense, and more funny, and more personal, and we're back to the status quo.

It's their own fault they've been stranded atop the wheel, which is a more compelling idea than it just breaking down. There's no rescue coming, they've been abandoned (there's an apt metaphor for their lives), and it's self-inflicted.

Of course they descend into talking bollocks, and making war film references.

When the supports break and send them swinging, it's genuinely terrifying.

This sets up a moment of self-reflection, as they face near-certain death, and even then they're being pervy.

Hole is the distilled essence of *Bottom* – Eau De Bottom – and is such a strong opening for the new series that the rest of it has a lot to live up to. That it was the final one to be recorded suggests that it may have been the original plan to make this the final episode. Maybe boring logic won the day, with the argument that the ending of *Carnival* meant it had to be the last one.

If *Carnival had* been the penultimate show, then a case could be made that *Hole* is Richie and Eddie stuck in purgatory, before they're given the chance to take stock and repent their sins, which they fail to do, and are then sent to Hell.

Nuggets

Hole was the final episode to be shot in the studio.

Since *Bottom: Live*, John Major had formally launched his Back To Basics campaign, the economy was growing (inflation was as a 30 year low of 1.6%), the Downing Street Declaration was signed, minister Tim Yeo resigned following a revelation he fathered a child with Julia Stent, more coal mines were closed, John Smith died and Tony Blair became leader of the Labour Party, the Conservatives suffered their worst election result of the century in the European elections, the IRA declared a ceasefire, unemployment fell, Neil Hamilton and Tim Smith became embroiled in the Cash For Question affair, and the National Lottery was launched.

As the credits roll, Richie and Eddie can be heard over the music, suggesting they have survived their fall.

Adrian's stunt double was Jeff Davis, and Rik's was Nick Wilkinson.

Hole was nominated for the prestigious Golden Rose award in Montreal, but lost out to *Don't Forget Your Toothbrush*.

In a webchat with *The Guardian*, Adrian reveals that his father used to say 'blood and stomach pills'.

There was a lot of comedy on this night in 1995. On BBC One, a repeat of *Only Fools And Horses* was followed by an episode of *Health And Efficiency*, a sort of sister show to *2point4 Children*. After *Bottom*, there was an episode of *The High Life*, and a repeat of *The Day Today*. Later you could watch *Fantasy Football League* and *Duckman*, while on ITV there was *The Upper Hand*, and Channel 4 had *Ellen, An Evening With Lee Evans, Roseanne, Whose Line Is It Anyway?*, and *Beavis And Butthead*.

Eddie, off screen, has blinded another stallholder, this time with a dart.

Unseen characters Keith and Deirdre are from the Lamb and Flag's Mixed Double's Nudey Tag Mud Wrestling Team. Keith is also known as One Legged Mad Dog Keith McFrenzy. Eddie has owed him £50 for seventeen years.

Eddie makes a rare mention of his father.

Richie's mother used to make sandwiches for the Hammersmith Conservative Association.

Eddie's newspaper, the *Hammersmith Bugle*, has a headline that reads 'No News Shocker' and has a story on the back page about 'Cup Tie Chaos'. The innards of the prop paper are made from the real pages of the *Surrey Herald*, with headlines including 'Rachel Enjoys A Sparkling Finish' and 'Seesaw Swans Hit Back'. This real paper was published on Thursday 3rd November 1994.

Unseen character, Grandpa Willis stole watches from corpses in the Somme.

Unseen character, Richie's sister, lives near the fair. Eddie apparently has never met her.

Unseen character Slip Digby is an organist. He also won the Stork margarine competition.

Eddie breaks the fourth wall, when he reveals they are atheists.

For this series, as the credits roll and the music plays, we also hear the studio audience listening along, sometimes clapping to the beat, and cheering.

TERROR

Written by Adrian Edmondson and Rik Mayall
Produced by Jon Plowman
Directed by Bob Spiers

Duration
29m07s

Recording Dates
Tuesday 4th – Wednesday 5th November 1994
Transmission Date
Friday 13th January 1995 at 9.00pm

Cast
Richie Richard – Rik Mayall
Eddie Hitler – Adrian Edmondson
Spudgun – Steven O'Donnell
Hedgehog – Christopher Ryan
Doreen Hedgehog – Lisa Coleman
Small Devil – Paul Ballar
Small Devil – Simon Coray
Small Devil – Mahommed George

BARB Ratings
5.22m (2nd)

Daily Mirror Blurb

*'It's Halloween and some trick-or-treaters get
a nasty surprise when they call upon Richie*

*(Rik Mayall) and Eddie (Ade Edmondson).
Inspired by this moneymaking idea, the
warring duo kit themselves out in fancy dress
and, armed with a cattle prod, go trick-or-
treating themselves.'*

Synopsis

It's breakfast time, and also a chance to check the
Spot The Ball competition. They haven't won, and
some kids arrive to Trick Or Treat at the front door.
Eddie refuses and gets a trident in the knackers as
a result.

Richie assumes it was an hallucination, and
concocts a hangover cure for Eddie, who drinks it
and passes out.

But they've had a brainwave, and later they too
are dressed for Trick Or Treating, brandishing a
cattle-prod which they will use to extort money
instead of chocolate. On the street, they get into a
fight with the kids, and lose, before knocking on
Spudgun's door.

They invite him to a party, and instruct him
to bring £2.50 as an entrance fee. Later, Richie
has decorated the flat and Eddie is making
homebrew. With no pumpkin, instead they've
made exploding carrots and some spicy sprouts.
Spudgun turns up, with Hedgehog in tow, and no
girls. In a pique of frustration,. Richie decides to
sell his soul to the Devil in exchange for sex and
money. They form a pentangle and show their
devotion to the devil by eating the evil sprouts.

They all pass out, and then the Devil knocks on the door, even if it's just Doreen, Hedgehog's daughter come to collect him. Relieved it's not the Devil after all, Spudgun relaxes a little too much, and excretes the sprout gas, igniting the exploding carrots.

Richie and Eddie have been pinning their hopes to a competition they don't actually understand. If that's not a metaphor for their lives, I don't know what is. *Terror* has a lot to live up to after *Hole*, but this is a good start – just the two of them at home, feeling downtrodden and overcompensating for it. They appear to have redecorated the flat (or the original set had been destroyed) – the walls are different, the conservatory/kitchen has a different layout, and the table has been replaced. There's even a different, weird photo of Elvis. It's not raining for once either, and is rather sunny. And even though there's lots of grease on the walls, it just doesn't feel as dank in there as it did.

On the other hand, the exterior set of the street is a tour de force. It looks fantastic, and is dressed perfectly. The old lamp posts, the bin bags, the layers of posters, the graffiti, the piles of dust in the gutter, the leaves atop the post box, and all the detritus in Spudgun's front yard really set the scene.

The more expansive nature of this episode, and a plethora of double-entendres and fart gags shows the other end of the spectrum from *Hole*, and while it speaks to *Bottom's* diversity of material (it's never just been toilet humour), there's a little too much over-reliance on it here in *Terror*.

But the little face Eddie draws on the carrot is so good that it even makes Ade corpse when he shows it off. It's one of those lovely touches that often goes unnoticed in *Bottom*.

Terror is a fun romp, and marks a change of tone from *Hole*, but suffers from following it for sure.

Nuggets

Terror was the second episode of series three to be recorded in the studio.

A poster remnant for Roger Taylor's album *Happiness* can be seen on the wall in the street. There's also one for The Jesus Mary Chain's *Sometimes Always*, and Maximum Carnage's *Paint The Town Red*. Elsewhere, there's a torn one for The Mandrake Theatre Company's production of *The Pistols*, and another for *Divine Intervention*. There's even a giant hoarding for Just Juice.

On BBC One this night, at 10.25pm, you could have watched *Peter Cook: The Best Of Not Only But Also*, a tribute to Cook who had died earlier in the week.

Lisa Coleman (who plays Doreen) is the sister of Charlotte Coleman.

Spudgun lives at number 9 of Chief Mangosuthu Buthelezi Cul-De-Sac.

Eddie breaks the fourth wall during the fight in the

alley with the devil kids.

There's a dog bowl marked 'Fido' under the couch.

Unseen character Ethel Cardew is now Eddie paramour, but she's not been speaking to him since the superglue incident.

BREAK

Written by Adrian Edmondson and Rik Mayall
Produced by Jon Plowman
Directed by Bob Spiers

Duration
28m**45**s

Recording Dates
Tuesday 25th – Wednesday 26th October 1994

Transmission Date
Friday 20th January 1995 at 9.00pm

Cast
Richie Richard – Rik Mayall
Eddie Hitler – Adrian Edmondson
Mormon – John Abbott
Voluptua – Jo-Anne Stockham

BARB Ratings
5.6m (3rd)

Daily Mirror Blurb

'Richie and Eddie plan a holiday, try home liposuction, pack their condoms and look forward to some action.'

Synopsis
Armed with tickets to a holiday in Bridlington,

Richie is massively excited and over-preparing for it. They are both hoping it will be as good as the last holiday when they caused a gas explosion and killed their landlady - but Richie's thong doesn't quite fit.

He need to lose some weight.

So they build an exercise device, using ropes and the fridge. When that doesn't really work, Eddie invents a running machine powered by his motorbike. That doesn't work as expected either, and sends Richie hurtling through the window. In retribution, Richie chainsaws Eddie's legs off.

They stitch them back on, and Richie panics that they might now miss their coach. He instructs Eddie to time the journey to the bus station, so Eddie grabs his darts and goes via the pub. When he gets back, he falls asleep on the sofa, drunk. Richie tries the fridge lifting machine once more, and gets trapped underneath it. Eddie comes to, having been faking it, and absconds with his friend Voluptua to enjoy their holiday together. He leaves Richie with a kick in the ghoulies.

Guff

The way the flat set is lit in series three – seemingly a lot brighter, in spite of the now very greasy windows – really does detract from the grot and squalor somehow.

Richie and Eddie forever getting excited about their holiday plans, even as they remember all the disasters from before, speaks to small embers of hope still glowing in their souls. But we know, and they must know, that it's only going to be the same thing over and over again. Especially now they're in hock for four grand.

In spite of that, Richie is bouncing with excitement. It's rather cute – as is their run on alternative to sun tan lotion (gloom juice). It's not often we see them in such a good mood. Until they suddenly realise their place in the world. Bottom is where they'll always be, so why not revel in a momentary bit of escape from it all?

Eddie doesn't appear to have learned much from his gas shenanigans, he exploded a guest house in much the same way as he did with Rottweiler's kitchen.

Break is a two-hander, set solely in the flat, and provides a very different character study than the others. It takes the excitement of an upcoming holiday, and makes us revel in the claustrophobia of the wait. Eddie's devious plot is a nice addition, and probably explains why he isn't quite so short-tempered with Richie. The episode explores the bleakness of hope, which is rather profound, and is hidden nicely among scenes of micro thongs, slapstick exercise machines, and chainsawing legs off.

Nuggets

Break was the fourth episode of the third series to be shot in the studio, and shared a pre-recording day with *Finger*.

Richie hums the *Match Of The Day* theme tune.

On the table is a milk bottle so old that its contents have separated into three distinct layers.

There's now two Elvis themed bits of tat on the organ. Wonder which of them is the fan ... and they keep their three-pack of Johnnies inside Elvis's head.

Unseen character Dodgy Bob McMayday is the most violent travel agent in the world.

There's a banana peel under the grill. Richie must have been foraging again. Also, there's an empty tube of toothpaste on top of the telly.

Unseen character Doctor Wildthroat is not a doctor of medicine.

Eddie breaks the fourth wall by nodding to camera after announcing he's about to make a deviously fiendish and mysterious phone call, and again when he makes his fantasy call to Cher. Later, he sneaks a worried look to camera after Richie nearly kisses him on the nob, and again, conspiratorially when Richie runs out of the flat.

There's an Othello themed board game on a shelf in the snug, called Apollo. On the same shelves are a couple of piles of tinsel. Elsewhere, in Richie's bedroom, amongst a pile of other games and jigsaws, he has the board game Harassment.

Richie and Eddie have a BAFTA award on their

bookshelf. God knows who Eddie mugged to get it. Later on in the episode, it has vanished.

Richie makes an extremely rare mention of his Dad. Turns out he too was absent, much like Eddie's – and was a Nazi spy in the war.

Eddie has a new paper – it's called *Bang* – and the headline beseeches us 'Don't Believe Tabloid Liars'.

When Eddie removes his coat from the hook, something large and heavy falls from it, and lands on the floor with an audible thunk. It's a shoe horn.

Eddie destroys another telly. This time it's during a drunken tirade of righteous indignation. When he falls and tears down the curtain, it reveals another couple of golden awards sitting on the sill.

Script Cuts/Deleted Scenes

On Fluff, there's a longer bit about the Desmond Lynam photo under the fridge, before Rik messes up his line.

DOUGH

Written by Adrian Edmondson and Rik Mayall
Produced by Jon Plowman
Directed by Bob Spiers

Duration
28m52s

Recording Dates
Tuesday 27th – Wednesday 28th September 1994
Transmission Date
Friday 27th January 1995 at 9.00pm

Cast
Richie Richard – Rik Mayall
Eddie Hitler – Adrian Edmondson
Spudgun – Steven O'Donnell
Hedgehog – Christopher Ryan
Dick Head – Lee Cornes
Nurse – Lucy Benjamin
CID Man – Peter Geeves
CID Man – Chris Sanders
CID Man – Raymond Sawyer
Student – Robert McKewley
Pub Man – Dominic Snowdon
Pub Man – Colin Wyatt
Skullcrusher – Nick Scott

BARB Ratings

6.09m (3rd)

Radio Times Blurb

'Who needs to win the National Lottery? Richie discovers that Eddie has a money-making scheme of his own.'

Synopsis

Richie fails once more to read any of *War And Peace*, and can't find anything else to do before sleep. And the noises coming from Eddie's bedroom are keeping him up anyway.

Wanting to know what's been going on in there for days, he spies through the keyhole, and is poked in the eye with a snooker cue for his troubles.

So when the doorbell rings, and desperate for company, he lets in Spudgun and Hedgehog and tries to chat to them, but they head straight to Eddie's room and leave Richie behind.

He finally gets inside, and discovers Eddie is forging money – badly. The plan is to distract people with the dirty imagery, then leg it before they're asked for real money.

They take the counterfeit cash to the Lamb And Flag, but Dick Head clocks it, and calls Skullcrusher Henderson. Offended that his own scam is being stolen, he demands five grand or else they get their skulls crushed.

In a stroke of coincidence, the prize for that night's pub quiz is exactly five grand.

So they head home to revise, and return with a

load of encyclopaedias which Richie hides in the lavs. Meanwhile, Eddie fiddles with the buzzers, so the other teams get electrocuted whenever they press them.

They actually win the quiz, and Dick Head hands over the cash.

But it's forged – by Henderson himself, and he proceeds to crush their skulls.

Guff

There's a C word joke that goes totally unnoticed by the audience at the beginning of *Dough* ('Well, they spelt the Count wrong, didn't they?'). And a nice moment where Richie, with complete honesty and self-awareness, says he's had no-one to talk at for ages.

We begin with a rare mystery, wondering exactly what Eddie's upto, as we watch Richie hump a fish bowl. He's bored, which usually means a caper plot is just round the corner. And what a wheeze it is, taking in Eddie's tortuous logic and infantile craft skills. He's gone from play telescopes to printing pornographic money. And his idea of porn is very odd indeed.

Once again, Spudgun and Hedgehog are a fun study in muted reactions as Richie whirls around them.

There's a lot of Rick in Richie when he's trying to join in and is being deliberately oblivious to the other's snubbing of him.

It's nice how their aspirations for the money go from Maserati's to a few free pints in the pub in just a few short minutes. Even with stacks of loot, they know they can't escape their lot really.

So it's not long before they get their comeuppance. After a brief win, they're now in hock to Skullcrusher, and fall for the scam (again), parting with gold teeth in order to win fake money.

Why do they keep going into the Lamb And Flag?

Nuggets

Dough was the first episode of the third season to be recorded.

Richie has finally finished reading *War And Peace*. Again.

Dick Head is wearing a Grenadier Guards tie.

Richie and Eddie must have sold their strange boom microphone to Dick, and it's casting lots of shadows around the pub.

Eddie gives a look and thumbs up to camera as he's beating Richie's head on the bar.

The dogs still bark whenever they enter the pub – that pheromone spray must be hardy.

Quiz teams include Hammersmith Hospital, Hammersmith C.I.D, The Dog And Handgun, and Hammersmith College – and Dick is taking questions from a box of cards marked '1000 Searching Question For 8-10 Year Olds.

The pub toilets are back to being maroon, and the graffiti has been painted over, apart from a single scrawled tag that seems to read as 'Edie'.

FINGER

Written by Adrian Edmondson and Rik Mayall
Produced by Jon Plowman
Directed by Bob Spiers

Duration
29m05s

Recording Dates
Tuesday 25th October – Wednesday 2nd November
1994
Transmission Date
Friday 3rd February 1995 at 9.00pm

Cast
Richie Richard – Rik Mayall
Eddie Hitler – Adrian Edmondson
Maitre 'D – Victor Spinetti
Marcel (Barman) – Kevin Allen
Maid – Caroline Gruber
Receptionist – Gareth Marks
Pierre – Rupert Rainsford
Woman In Toilet – Sue Scott-Davison

BARB Ratings
6.09m (6th)

Daily Mirror Blurb

'When Eddie and Richie steal a car and find

Synopsis

Upon returning from a Stag Cricket match, Richie learns that it was a present to let the groom beat Richie unconscious. Eddie also reveals that he's nicked the groom's car keys, so Richie plots his revenge.

They steal the car, and in doing so discover the honeymoon tickets.

And so Eddie and Richie head for the hotel, posing as the happy couple, and take the honeymoon themselves. The subterfuge requires Eddie to dress as a woman, and the Barman finds him very attractive. Eddie is flattered, and Richie is offended that his new bride is flirting back. A fight ensues, and the groom arrives to exact his own revenge with a cricket ball.

Guff

Finger was never my favourite instalment of *Bottom*, with its mix of *Some Like It Hot* and the British sitcom tradition of a holiday episode. It starts with a great visual gag though, what with Eddie covered in jumpers and hats, and the red streak on Richie's trousers suggesting he was a little too vigorous with the old ball polishing.

The opening scene is fun, hearing them discuss antics that happened off-screen always is, and Richie and Eddie doing post-match analysis races along. It's a nice way to set up the revenge plot too. The street set is another tour de force. Not only does it look great, it looks lived in, and is once again brilliantly dressed. There's even a man moving around in the off-licence at the back.

It's also fun, and funny, how absurd the driving sequence looks, and the Ford Capri is well-chosen.

The hotel itself looks like something straight out of *Keeping Up Appearances*, right down to the wallpaper. It screams mid 1990s, and is about the only set in the whole series to do this. The business men in the background are doing some terrible acting, by the way. They are dressed for the 90s too. There's something a bit odd about seeing Richie and Eddie in such time specific environs, and maybe that's one of the reasons this episode feels wonky.

Eddie in a dress seems like a last resort idea, and that's my biggest gripe with *Finger* – but they do some vaguely interesting things with it. Eddie getting a taste of his own medicine for example, and how quickly he adopts the feminist cause (even if for nefarious purposes). Richie is as creepy as he's ever been when interacting with the maid, and doesn't really get much comeuppance for it.

Eddie's quacking pipe is a lovely touch.

But all in all, for an episode with such a promising opening couple of scenes, it just loses its way really.

Nuggets

Finger was the fifth episode of the third series to

be shot. It shared its pre-record day with *Break* though, when they shot the car stunt, and the first two scenes, probably to make way for the hotel sets. The rest of the episode's pre-recording was conducted on the morning of that evening's audience recording.

Kevin Allen is Keith Allen's brother.

The Fido dog bowl is now in the corner between the two doors.

The milk on the table is now so old it's separated into four layers.

Unseen character Cannonball Taffy O'Jones is a violent bowler, and got married to a woman who looks like Ted Rogers.

Unseen character Old Ted Unlucky Suicide McGloomy was seen to be laughing at Richie's accident, causing his rectum to prolapse.

The off-licence is called Cork And Bottle, and is next door to North And Sons, the estate agents on one side, and Auto Sounds on the other.

The Marvelloso Splendido Hotel sounds a lot like a certain guest house. It's in Wolverhampton.

Producer Jon Plowman plays the bellhop.

Caroline Gruber, the maid, also appeared in the notorious BSB sitcom *Heil Honey, I'm Home.*

We learn why Richie reacted the way he did when he ate the Sunday Fish Finger – Eddie has a habit of hollowing them out and filling them with dog shit.

CARNIVAL

Written by Adrian Edmondson and Rik Mayall
Produced by Jon Plowman
Directed by Bob Spiers

Duration
29m04s

Recording Dates
Tuesday 11th – Wednesday 12th October 1994
Transmission Date
Friday 10th February 1995 at 9.00pm

Cast
Richie Richard – Rik Mayall
Eddie Hitler – Adrian Edmondson

BARB Ratings
6.91m (2nd)

Daily Mirror Blurb

'Richie loots a camcorder during a riot and hauls Eddie in to make a TV show.'

Synopsis

It's the annual Hammersmith Riot, and Eddie and Richie have the best seats in the house, watching the carnage from their window. Enthused by what they see, they head down to do some looting themselves, and return with a meagre haul. But Richie has managed to nick a camera from the BBC news crew.

Eddie acts as cameraman, while Richie puts together a demo for a current affairs show, but ends up falling down the stairs instead. They realise there may be money to be won from staging accidents for Jeremy Beadle.

They fake some, but the camera was never rolling – which is the best accident yet, and should definitely earn them a few hundred quid. Eddie sets up the video to check that the tape is indeed blank, but it turns out to contain incriminating footage of the Prime Minister.

They try to extort him, but the SAS arrive and surround the flat.

Richie and Eddie issue their demands, which are not met, and instead the SAS storm in and gun them down in an homage to Blake's 7.

Guff

Carnival manages to feel large and expansive without ever leaving the flat. The carnival is well-realised through lighting, smoke, and sound design. There aren't many sitcoms that would have a tight two shot of their characters just talking, with few cutaways, for nearly six minutes. And it's a nice touch to have this shot echo the opening titles.

The argument about the duck is pure *Bottom*, twisted logic and all, and the way it morphs into a pantomime of shopping is a fun subversion of the trope – the idle chit chat of looting. It's also a great misdirect for the burglary, and the irony of their indignation at being robbed.

When Richie extracts himself from the lavatory, he looks an awful lot like Donald Trump.

There's something weirdly delightful about two masters of slapstick dissecting what is and isn't funny about physical humour, making a clear distinction between real life pain and cartoon pain. We see Eddie in actual agony after their staging it for the camera, something we never normally see on *Bottom*. Injuries are usually there for the laughs. There's also some commentary hidden in there about the toll of physical humour, and having to do multiple takes.

Then, for the first time in this third series, rain lashes at the windows, and the flat seems like its old self again, even if the gloom doesn't last long.

Eddie does a remarkably good impression of John Major.

I remember being genuinely shocked at their apparent deaths at the end of this episode, but it's wonderful that it's never explained away.

If you don't buy that *Bottom* is rooted in the politics of post-Thatcher Britain, and is a commentary on the new beginnings of moralistic politics, bear in mind that the one thing that could elevate Richie and Eddie out of their shackles - a tape of John Major being exposed as immoral, while head of a party that held on to power with a Back To Basics agenda - a tape that could bring down that government - they are *within seconds* descended upon and gunned to death.

The angry hope of youth, of *The Young Ones*, has given way to the nihilism of middle age. No matter what they do, Richie and Eddie will always be at the bottom, lying in the sewer and gazing up hopelessly at the stars.

Nuggets

Carnival was the third episode of the third series to be shot.

After this episode ended, BBC Two ran a 2-minute segment called *Two's Comedy* as part of the run up to *Comic Relief*. It was a phone poll about the nation's favourite comedy moments. This one was a duel between Alan Partridge singing on *Knowing Me Knowing You*, and *The Young Ones* appearing on *University Challenge*.

After the series ended, it was replaced by repeats of *Steptoe And Son*.

We learn that Amal, who owns the Kebab shop opposite the flat, is nicknamed 'Fatty'.

Unseen character Father O'Malley owns a gun, and enjoys shooting it whilst drunk and naked.

The kebab shop opposite the flat, which they watch burn down, now inexplicably has a hoarding announcing it as an Off Licence.

Not only is Eddie under the illusion that Tony Blair is a woman, he also believes him to be his MP. Eddie does not live in Sedgefield.

The Fido dog bowl is back under the couch.

Eddie shoots a look down the lens when Richie announces he's going to make his own current affairs discussion programme, and again when Richie says it's the 80s after all.

Script Cuts/Deleted Scenes

On *Fluff*, we see Ade offering different takes on what's been thrown through Curry's window. It goes from a policeman, to a nun, to Aswad.

BOTTOM LIVE: THE BIG NUMBER 2 TOUR

Written by Adrian Edmondson and Rik Mayall
Produced by Phil McIntyre
Directed by Dominic Brigstocke
Presented by Phil McIntyre

Duration
1h50m

Tour Dates (all 1995)
Monday 18 – Saturday 23 September
– Bristol Hippodrome
Monday 25 – Wednesday 27 September
– Woking New Victoria Theatre
Thursday 28 – Friday 29 September
– Wolverhampton Civic Hall
Sunday 1 and Tuesday 3 October
– Bournemouth B.I.C
Monday 2 October – Portsmouth Guildhall
Wednesday 4 – Friday 6 October
– Plymouth Pavilions
Monday 9 – Thursday 12 October – Oxford Apollo

Monday 16 – Tuesday 17 October – Brighton Dome
Wednesday 18 October – Manchester Apollo
Thursday 19 – Saturday 21 October
– Edinburgh Festival Theatre
Monday 23 – Wednesday 25 October
– Glasgow Concert Hall
Friday 27 – Saturday 28 October
– Portsmouth Guildhall
Monday 30 October – Saturday 4
November – Leeds Grand Theatre
Monday 6 – Saturday 11 November
– Birmingham Hippodrome
Sunday 12 – Tuesday 14 November
– Cardiff St David's Hall
Thursday 16 – Saturday 18 November
– Manchester Apollo
Sunday 19 November – Nottingham
Royal Concert Hall
Monday 20 November – Leicester De Montfort Hall
Friday 24 – Saturday 25 November –
Blackburn King George's Hall
Sunday 26 – Tuesday 28 November
– Newcastle City Hall
Wednesday 29 November – Hull City Hall
Friday 1 – Monday 3 December -
Wolverhampton Civic Hall
Wednesday 5 – Thursday 6 December
– Sheffield City Hall
Friday 7 – Sunday 10 December –
Hammersmith Labbat's Apollo
Monday 11 – Thursday 14 December

– Liverpool Empire
Monday 18 December – Scarborough
Futurist Theatre
Tuesday 19 – Wednesday 20 December
– Nottingham Royal Centre

Recording Dates
Monday 9 – Thursday 12 October 1995
at the Oxford Apollo Theatre

Original Release Dates
Monday 6th November 1995

VHS/DVD/Audio Cassette Back Matter

The first Bottom Live was squalid, violent and downright hilarious. The Big Number 2 Show is all that and more.

Filmed during the 1995 sell-out nationwide tour that left over 500,000 fans standing on their seats and screaming for more. The Big Number 2 Show features Adrian Edmondson as Eddie and Rik Mayall as Richie at their most demonic, violent and uncensored best.

The problem is sex! From the Queen to a sheep, they desperately and catastrophically try to press the flesh at every available opportunity whilst farting, fighting and cursing their way through their disgusting and sleazy lives.

Bottom Live 'The Big Number 2 Show', is the

funniest and most outrageous comedy you will ever see. Grab your Bottom now.

Cast
Richie – Rik Mayall
Eddie – Adrian Edmondson

Synopsis

The Queen is going to visit, which massively over-excites Richie, while Eddie keeps forgetting because he is permanently drunk. They think it will be a good idea if, during her tour of Mafeking Parade, they get their todgers out and set off a load of fireworks.

They are sentenced to 350 years in prison.

While incarcerated, Richie attracts the unwanted attention of Geoffrey Nasty, and so they plan and execute their escape. To defend themselves back at home, they booby trap the flat, but the Queen has come for tea, and they accidentally kill her and themselves.

Reviews

'Topical Witty Bottom Is The Tops

Last week saw the return to Plymouth of Rik Mayall and Adrian Edmondson for their West Country leg of Bottom, The Big Number Two tour! Already an award-winning TV series, the adaptation to stage was brilliant. The two-hour performance to a capacity Pavilions audience was classic with Rik and Ade at their witty and violent best. Full of sound and lighting effects, the show was fast-paced and incredibly funny - both visually and verbally - with an excellent, topical script. Rumour is that this is the last tour, and should that be true, the boys certainly know how to go out with a bang!'

(JP, PLYMOUTH EXTRA, 12TH OCTOBER 1995)

'Rik Mayall and Adrian Edmondson go together in much the same way as Tony Hancock and Sid James did 30 years ago. The difference is that the pair, alias Richie Rich and Eddie Hitler, are violent, crude, filthy and sex-obsessed. Filmed at the Oxford Apollo, this irreverent tour de force targets the Queen, Gloria Hunniford, an unfortunate parrot and anyone else available.'

(HERTS AND ESSEX OBSERVER, 16TH NOVEMBER 1995)

'"Eddie get downstairs and unload my vegetables"

Rik Mayall and Adrian Edmondson have lived toilet humour together for over 15 years and it still seems to be working.

This opening gambit, after the strains of Richie groaning through the mike, welcomes us to Bottom - The Big Number Two Tour, a new two-hour set from the award winning TV series, which ran on Tuesday and last night, completing the 81 -date tour.

Both nights sold out months in advance and as Rik Mayall and Adrian Edmondson appear on stage there's a heroes' welcome - to such an extent that it becomes part of the whole show. As they make their garbled, silly noises they see who can get the biggest reaction from the audience.

We're in Richie and Eddie's flat in Hammersmith at a reasonable hour of the morning. It's a filthy affair befitting of their obsession with all things dirty.

Richie (Mayall) is the sadder of the two, obsessed with sex - but ever failing - a slimy, sad character with his shirt tucked into his high-riding underpants. Eddie is the dominant one and out for what he can get - but still shares the no-hoper tag with Richie.

There's a basic plot around the two's slapstick violence, cursing, belching, and sex gags, whereby The Queen is due to visit and Richie has decided that he will lose his long-standing virginity to her. With a storyline like that it proves they haven't lost the ability to go over the edge - keeping the smut rich but somehow innocently boyish.

Apart from that there are no surprises in store. It's typical toilet teamwork and judging by the reaction exactly what we wanted.

And it's a well-crafted show, full of perfectly timed 'ad-libs' which the audience seem to fall for every time. References to Nottingham are a-plenty: "It's no good pretending to be Robin Hood" says Edmondson "You're looking more like Friar Tuck these days" referencing Mayall's noticeable weight increase.

Towards the end though, the 'mistakes' seem to become a bit too obvious. But nobody cares - scripted or not it's still funny.

To the second scene in a prison cell, the sound-effect violence continues, as do the references to sex and numerous bodily functions.

Edmondson has revealed that this is their very last show of Bottom. No more stage shows, no more television.

"We've decided to stop it, we've had enough" he said.

"We couldn't think of anything we hadn't already done. The last series was by far the best and the next series would be fine but not any better. Nottingham has the Bottom end."

That's a shame for lovers of laddish slapstick, which is an ancient art but still very funny and very popular. However, it seems to be so ingrained in their nature, they'll no doubt be back for more.'

(SIMON WILSON, NOTTINGHAM EVENING POST, 21ST DECEMBER 1995)

Guff

Physically locking Richie and Eddie in a prison cell together seems like the logical conclusion of *Bottom's* theme. So to get them there, you might as well have them commit treason. They're trapped together anyway, so it makes sense to trap them together forever.

Even The Samaritans hang up on Richie these days, and their luck is so bad that they can only win a lottery they're the sole participants in.

The Queen coming to tea is a nice mystery that's left unexplained for a while, which makes the first act a leisurely stroll with these two characters. Some of the things we've learned that arouse them are bizarre, none more so than Richie calling Zippy from *Rainbow* a horn monster.

The Oxford Apollo audience seems a bit subdued, though they do often erupt into rapturous applause breaks. Rik and Ade really are working hard here, so might as well end the first act on a bang.

The audience is much more lively at the start of the second half – or maybe each half is from different performances.

I wonder if the prison thing is a deliberate reference to the play *Cell Mates*, infamous as playing a part in Stephen Fry's disappearance, or if it's entirely coincidental.

Either way, it's a nice bit of stage design to have the cell simply sit inside the flat set.

Once again Richie and Eddie spend a lot of time recounting how they've ended up in their latest predicament. It's funnier to hear about these things than see them, especially with the added colour of the character's attitudes towards them. Eddie is resigned and bored, Richie full of bluster. The two of them in a courtroom scene might have been fun at some point in the series though.

It's very clever how they hide the gas emitters around the cell set.

In a rare bit of luck, they actually manage to escape, but for some reason, head straight back home. It's like an instinct for them, they know where they belong.

Nuggets

Adrian makes reference to Stephen Fry's disappearance when he was co-starring alongside Rik in *Cell Mates*, a play by Simon Grey, in February of 1995.

In the short time since the end of series three, the manufacturing sector reported its biggest rise in unemployment for sixteen years (though wider employment was improving), Barings Bank collapsed, the Conservatives lost big in the local elections, there was an outbreak of Mad Cow Disease, and John Major resigned as leader of his party (triggering a leadership election that he then won).

The electrocution helmet from the first live show can be seen on a cabinet in the living room.

This is technically the last time we see the drawing room and kitchen set, since none of the remaining live shows feature it.

During promotional interviews for this tour, in particular for the *Nottingham Evening Post* at the end of the run (and with Sarah Greene on *Pebble Mill*), Adrian announces that this will be the last instalment of *Bottom*, there will be no more live shows, and no other series. He also talks about his new novel The Gobbler, and hints that he and Rik are making a TV movie in the vein of Laurel And Hardy.

Rik enjoys starting live shows from off-stage. He often did this on his solo tours.

Richie shops at Kwik Save.

It's true, Richie's Freeman's catalogue really does

fall open on the lingerie page.

They have a new couch, and a new piece of furniture where the book shelf usually is. A nice mid-century dresser for the birdcage to sit on.

Unseen character Geoffrey Nasty is a psychopathic penis remover who owns a tortoise. Later, in prison, he works for another unseen character, Horace Big.

The *Hammersmith Bugle* announces 'No News Again Nightmare'.

Unseen characters Michael O'Hooligan and Patricia O'Violence sold Eddie some Semtex. Their friend, Pat O'Cake, is a baker's man.

Mr Rottweiler, the neighbour has moved out. Now their neighbour is foul-mouthed Mrs Tiggywinkle.

Unseen character Mad Dog Patrick Do You Want Some Of This O'Fist beat Richie up after Eddie stole his Guinness.

Eddie's Great Uncle Susan fell unconscious on a stock of mustard gas. Eddie also has an Uncle Stalin.

On the cell wall is a Nolan's poster, perhaps a reference to *Filthy Rich And Catflap*.

In a Q and A for *The Guardian*, Ade admits the missing watch gag is faked. It started, and was embellished, once when Rik really had forgotten his watch. In the same Q and A, he also reveals that abandoned scripts for a fourth TV series were bowdlerised for the subsequent live shows.

Unseen character Mad Quentin Trousers Down Pervy O'Blimey once used a toilet in the Star Of Burma Kebab And Peepshow on the Uxbridge Road during the Gulf War.

More fun dual credits such as Tour Manager/Chauffeur, Production Manager/Queen, Lighting Designer/Moving Light Fan, Special Effect/Cider Finder, and Truck Driver/Merchandise.

BOTTOM LIVE 3: HOOLIGAN'S ISLAND

Written by Adrian Edmondson and Rik Mayall
Produced by Phil McIntyre and Paul Roberts
Directed by Ed Bye
Presented by Phil McIntyre

Duration
1h40m

Tour Dates (all 1997)
Monday 13 – Saturday 18 January –
Nottingham Royal Centre
Monday 20 – Saturday 25 January –
Labatt's Apollo Manchester
Monday 27 January – Saturday 1
February – Sheffield City Hall
Monday 3 – Saturday 8 February
– Liverpool Empire
Monday 10 – Saturday 15 February
– Glasgow King's Theatre
Monday 17 – Saturday 22 February
– Bradford Alhambra

Monday 24 February – Saturday 1
March – Oxford Apollo
Sunday 2 March – Saturday 8 March
– Birmingham Hippodrome
Monday 10 – Thursday 13 March – Ipswich Regent
Friday 14 – Saturday 15 March –
Blackpool Opera House
Monday 17 – Saturday 22 March
– Bristol Hippodrome

Recording Dates
17th March – 22nd March 1997 at
the Bristol Hippodrome

Original Release Dates
Monday 27th October 1997

VHS/DVD/Audio Cassette Back Matter

Bottom Live 3 – Hooligan's Island is the biggest, best, funniest and most outrageous live show ever!

Rik Mayall and Adrian Edmondson are back – even bigger and more Bottomly than ever – with Bottom Live 3 Hooligan's Island. Filmed during their sell-out 1997 tour we find Richie and Eddie marooned on a desert island in the middle of the Pacific.

Will they build a raft and escape? Grasp the opportunity to embrace the earthly paradise around them? Or will they simply bicker and fart, fight, puke, poke and masturbate their way through 100 minutes of the most hilariously outrageous live situation comedy on offer in Britain today?

Bottom Live 3 – Hooligan's Island is uncensored, obscene, violent and unbelievably hilarious.

Cast
Richie – Rik Mayall
Eddie – Adrian Edmondson

Synopsis

Richie and Eddie have been stranded on an uncharted island for three years, and this morning Richie finds himself trapped in the lav. Once free, and having administered the Shag Of Life to an albatross, he begins to make breakfast. The fish he found in the latrine doesn't go down well, and after he has evacuated himself, they hear the drumbeat of nearby Welsh cannibals who are cooking Keith Floyd in a giant pot. Richie and Eddie are spotted, hunted, and shot at with poison darts. Eddie saves Richie's life with an antidote he's found in a nearby Japanese World War Two bunker.

As he recuperates, the duo recount the tale of how they ended up on the island – it involved Ecstasy, a police chase, and hijacking an ambulance, before swapping favours for a job performing on a cruise ship. Their act set the ship on fire, and Eddie's efforts to dowse the flames caused it to sink. They stayed afloat by clinging on to Eddie's organ, and six hours later they were washed ashore on the island.

As act two begins, they are still awaiting their rescue, until they uncover a 15 megaton nuclear bomb, left behind by the French, and accidentally activate it. Their efforts to defuse the bomb fail, but they see a passing French naval ship. Eddie tries to signal it with a flare, but the flare destroys the ship, and the bomb explodes.

Reviews

'Dirty Duo Have Lost Their Spark

The last time the Bottom show came to town - just over a year ago at the end of the Big Number Two Tour - Adrian Edmondson exclusively revealed to the Post that it was the end for Richie and Eddie. No more shows, no more tours.

After last night's opening performance of Bottom Live 3: Hooligan's Island - running all week at the Royal Concert Hall - a less polite critic might suggest that perhaps they should have called it a day.

Don't get me wrong, the first two tours were superb – filthy, childish and hilarious.

Rik Mayall and Adrian Edmondson are

probably the only alternative comedians not to have mellowed over the years and dipped into the mainstream. For that they are to be saluted.

Of course, last night the trademark toilet humour - which has kept them going for 16 years - was there.

As was the slapstick violence and digs at Robin Hood.

Comedy sophisticates would grind their teeth at the success of their textbook humour - but that would be missing the point.

And of course, there's hardly any storyline to speak of - they are marooned on a desert island for three years, Richie has the runs, Eddie has a secret stash of spirits, they fend off cannibals with vomit, Richie kills an albatross, the French dump a nuclear bomb on the island, that's it.

But it wasn't a story that was missing - more the spark, the spontaneity, the enthusiasm.

Mind you, with such a successful formula, critical success probably means very little to the duo.

*The six Nottingham dates have all sold out -
in fact the whole tour has sold out.*

*The duo received a rousing welcome as
the audience largely enjoyed two hours of
humour from the Bottom.*

*There's no doubt they are at their best when
making mistakes, whether scripted or not.
Mayall fluffs his lines on a regular basis and
plays up to it, so you can't help wondering.*

*Mind you, one mistake I'm sure wasn't
supposed to happen was the closing curtain
fall - usually a less than polite stage-sized
request to "go away" - which last night was
back to front and therefore illegible.*

*If you are going to see Bottom this week,
have a drink beforehand and don't expect too
much.'*

(SIMON WILSON, NOTTINGHAM EVENING POST, 14TH JANUARY 1997)

Guff

As the collective hope of the United Kingdom rose, and the strains of *Things Can Only Get Better* rang out before the next general election – there's was no way that Richie and Eddie could be allowed that hope. Whether or not they truly would have been yanked up from their bottoms isn't the point – that they could have that legitimate expectation was anathema to their situation.

And so, we find them stranded on a tropical island that's about to be consumed by a nuclear explosion (maybe there's a political metaphor in that).

The island looks great on stage, brightly lit, and almost inviting. They could have made it as a sort of strung together pantomime of the flat, but they resisted that urge, perhaps for the better. And it was designed by Rik and Ade according to the credits, and built by Russell Beck Studios.

Rik's doing a slightly different voice for Richie at the beginning, a more theatrical version of it (there's a croak to it too, from vocal strain), which feels more like an impression to begin with, and makes relaxing back into the character a little more work. It slips back to normal later.

Richie's still deluding himself that he's officer material, even as he has to crap in a sandy hole.

Eddie seems to be having a great time, plus he's managed to keep his hat. His first kick to Richie's face is immaculately realised. And let's take a moment to appreciate the remarkable timing of the sound effects in these live shows. It's pretty audacious to take so long to address their being on the island too.

There appears to be some cut material when they're looking at the fish in the frying pan. As silly as the whole bit about the fish and Richie's bowels is, it's some cleverly stealthy exposition about what's going on with the island.

When Richie emerges from the latrine with his trousers down, Ade hands Rik something behind his back, or maybe he's adjusting his microphone pack.

As Richie beseeches Eddie to think of something that will help thwart the poison, a lone voice in the audience shouts 'have a wank'. It gets no reaction.

Eddie's good mood turns on an albatross excretion, and he reaches his own bottom now, yearning for 'the good old days' of Hammersmith and *Supermarket Sweep*. Then we hear the tale of how they ended up marooned, and it's pretty epic.

Richie and Eddie have some amazing adventures off-screen.

Shame they've enhanced the end of act explosion with some dodgy VFX.

Richie saying 'bam-boo' reminds me of Tim Conway's running gag pronunciation of 'koala' on *The Carol Burnett Show*.

Rik is a remarkably good mimic.

The start of this act sees them reverting to their more usual dynamic, with the boredom and the tension rising, even as a giant bomb sits behind them unnoticed. They can't even find peace on a tropical island.

And when they are offered an escape, they resort to idiotic xenophobia instead. That sounds all too familiar these days. The Little England mentality of these characters is morphing now into something even more insidious, and we're not meant to be on their side. Once more, *Bottom* does politics by stealth. They're dressing up their failures and predicament in nationalism, the way they've been taught to. Stops them focusing on the real reasons.

Nuggets

The title is of course a reference to *Gilligan's Island*.

Since the *Big Number 2 Tour*, Britain saw the privatisation of the railways, the divorce of Charles and Diana, the Arms To Iraq Affair, falling unemployment, and a huge Tory defeat in local elections with a General Election just around the corner.

The note that reads 'Iranu uvavu' is a nod to *Shooting Stars*, and the sounds heard during the Dove From Above round (and its various iterations).

The wire work to make Ade fly was done by Flying By Foys.

The tour clothing was supplied by Woolrich.

The souvenir programme consisted of a rip-off calendar for 1997.

Ed Bye returns to direct *Bottom* for the first time since *'S Out*.

On 23rd August 2012, BBC Two announced that a series based on *Hooligan's Island* had been commissioned:

> *'Next year it will be 18 years since Richard*

Richard "Richie Richard" Richard and Eddie Hitler last graced our television screens.

Long enough for a generation to be born, learn to walk and talk, grow up, go to school, nearly learn to read, leave school and register for job seekers' allowance all without having experienced the wit and wisdom of two of comedy's greatest characters.

All that is about to change as we find out what happened to two titans of comedy, Richie and Eddie. Are they still wandering round and round Hammersmith roundabout looking for a safe place to cross? Are they still living in one of the dirtiest and least hygienic flats uncondemned by Health and Safety? Are they still drinking neat furniture polish whilst hitting each other over the head with large metal objects, setting fire to each other's private parts and other areas as they seek to impress gullible members of the opposite sex, and each other? Or are they down the pub?

No, they are abandoned, lost and shipwrecked on a tropical hell hole that is Hooligans' Island, although they are still hitting each other over the head with large metal objects, still chasing women, (even though there are none on the island) and still waiting for that job seekers' allowance cheque as they distil something quite like alcohol, only worse.

And they are back on BBC Two in 2013 for six new 30-minute episodes starring Rik Mayall and Ade Edmondson. Be afraid. Be very afraid. And a bit bilious.

Rik Mayall says: "How much am I getting paid? Are there any birds in it? And that horrific arse-brained Edmondson's not in it again is he? Oh, God help me... no, no, alright then, I'll do it. That useless, foul smelling waste of space and oxygen is really going to get it this time. This is the big one. Tell the audience to brace themselves."

*Ade Edmondson said: "It's been a while since I last worked with that complete b****** Rik Mayall and I'm very much looking forward to bashing him about the head with various blunt objects. It's the only language he understands."*

Commissioned by Janice Hadlow, Controller, BBC Two and Mark Freeland, Head of BBC In-House Comedy, Hooligans' Island will be a BBC Comedy co-production with Phil McIntyre Television. It will be executive produced by Mark Freeland and produced by Jon Plowman.'

(BBC PRESS RELEASE, 23RD AUGUST 2012)

But by the middle of October, the project had been cancelled, as Adrian announced on BBC Radio Essex:

> *'I'm aware that people think comedy's easy to do and write and everything, and it relatively is to be honest. But once you get to a certain age you want to do things you really enjoy, not just things you can do.'*

Unseen character Sir Pervy Leslie McBlowjob is a theatrical impresario.

Once again, we see that Eddie can't even spell his own name, with his sign that says 'Edie's Bra'.

GUEST HOUSE PARADISO

Written by Adrian Edmondson and Rik Mayall
Directed by Adrian Edmondson
Produced by Phil McIntyre

Duration
1h29m

Release Date
Friday 3rd December 1999

VHS/DVD Back Matter

'Bottom with knobs on' NME

Bottom explodes onto the big screen with a bang, crash and a scream!

Richie and Eddie are running the nastiest, smelliest, most squalid hotel in the world and things aren't going well. The Chef's guzzled all the food, cash is running low and most of the guests have fled without paying!

But things are on the up with the arrival of the Nice family, some exotic underwear and the sexy Italian move star Gina Carbonara. Richie is soon indulging his passion for panty pilfering whilst desperately trying to impress the fragrant Ms. Carbonara! But with Gina's jilted fiancée in hot pursuit and something decidedly iffy about the fish dinner Richie and Eddie are going to need a miracle to escape in one piece.

'Mindless and hysterically funny' Uncut

Cast
Richard Twat – Rik Mayall
Eddie Elizabeth Ndindombaba
– Adrian Edmondson
Mr Johnson – Bill Nighy
Mrs Hardy – Kate Ashfield
Chef – Steven O'Donnell
Mrs Foxfur – Fenella Fileding
Newscaster – Charles Cartmell
Gino Bolognese – Vincent Cassel
Gina Carbonara – Helene Mahieu
Saucy Wood Nymph – Sophia Myles
Saucy Wood Nymph – Emma Pierson
Saucy Wood Nymph - Anna Madeley
Mr Nice – Simon Pegg
Mrs Nice – Lisa Palfrey
Damien Nice – Joseph Hughes
Charlene Nice – Jessica Mann
Truck Driver #1 – Richard Hammatt
Young Groom – James D'Arcy

Young Bride – Kate Loustau
Chatty Worker – Bob Mason
Sickly Worker – Phillip Lester
Worried Worker – Richard Strange
Intimidating Man – David Sibley

Richie Twat and Eddie Ndindombaba run one of the worst hotels in the country. It stands next to a nuclear power station, and is staffed by drunks and idiots. What's more, Richie is rude to the guests, and they are conning the senile Mrs Foxfur out of her money.

But the latest guests to arrive throw a spanner in the works. First, there's the Nice family, who can't afford to holiday anywhere else, and then Italian movie star Gina Carbonara shows up, wanting to hide from her abusive fiancé.

With the chef unable to cook, it's left to Richie and Eddie to do the catering, and they're cooking some fish that fell off the back of a lorry. Literally. It was being taken away by the military because it's been poisoned by a radioactive leak from the power plant.

Gino Bolognese arrives, looking for his fiancée, and eats some of the fish. As do all the guests, except Gina, and there's an outbreak of violent, projectile vomiting that ends up killing Gino. Richie and Eddie attempt to flee the scene with Gina, only to be confronted by Government agents. To silence them, and cover up the incident, they're given £10 million, new identities, and first class tickets to the

Caribbean.

'Mayall and Edmondson are Richie Twat (pronounced Thwaite) and Eddie Elizabeth Ndingombaba (unpronounceable), owners of the Guest House Paradiso, a damp-ridden hellhole on the edge of a cliff and adjacent to a nuclear power station. Business is slow, but that all changes when world famous movie star Gina Carbonara (Mahieu) arrives to seek refuge from her hotheaded boyfriend.

Rik Mayall and Adrian Edmondson's film careers have been neither prolific nor particularly successful and, as everyone knows they do their best stuff when they work together, they have sensibly chosen one of their most popular television creations, the fabulous Bottom, to go all cinematic.

But the plot, as with the TV show, is irrelevant. This is Mayall's and Edmondson's domain, as they skip from their trademark brand of extreme violence to, well, more of it. Of course, it does rather depend on whether you are a fan of the two leads and their particular style, which while often mirthsome, is undoubtedly puerile and sometimes tasteless. There are some smart cameos, especially Pegg as a weedy guest, *but when the puke inspired denouement does finally arrive, it feels over-baked and stretched out. Much like the rest of the movie.*

The boys toil incredibly hard to make the whole thing work and, while there are some hilarious moments, it is far too patchy for a full feature film.'

(BEN FALK, EMPIRE)

'Big Screen First For Bottom Duo

It is, perhaps surprisingly, the first time that Rik Mayall and Adrian Edmondson have stepped up to the big screen together, as the Bottom TV show collides roughly with Fawlty Towers and a big old frantic mess results.

As you would expect, the film is loud, full-on slapstick - in which the slaps are mostly replaced by punches, kicks and knees to the dangly areas - all perpetrated with considerable speed, enthusiasm and energy.

And, remarkable as it may seem, operates very much like a Merchant Ivory film: a genre-specific product to be viewed by a fully paid-up fanbase and treated with some caution by everybody else.'

(LIVERPOOL ECHO, 3RD DECEMBER 1999)

'Richie Twat (Rik Mayall), pronounced Thwaite, and Eddie Ndingombaba (Adrian Edmondson) run the world's worst hotel.

It perches on a remote cliff edge, bang next door to a leaky nuclear power station.

In this Fawlty Towers-from-Hell, the disreputable duo manage to insult and/ or drive away every guest. Yet even they are a bit stretched for new indignities after the arrival incognito of Italian movie babe Gina Carbonara (Helene Mahieu) and her dangerously volatile boyfriend Gino Bolognese (Vincent Cassel).

Fans of Rik-and-Ade will, of course, know exactly what to expect – much vomiting, violent slapstick and, freed from the restraints of television, copious four-letter words and sexual crudity.

But, while pacy TV shows like Bottom or The Young Ones can work brilliantly, this extended sketch becomes painfully overstretched at 86 minutes and the laughter wears very thin.'

(SUNDAY MIRROR, 5TH DECEMBER 1999)

'As an exercise in the relentless accretion

of grossness, Guest House Paradiso is so in love with filth it makes There's Something About Mary look like The Importance of Being Earnest. But it's impossible not to have some sort of aghast admiration for this film's single-minded devotion to the lower portions of the human body. Six-year-old boys of all ages will love it. Alongside Guest House Paradiso's swirling tides of piss, phlegm, blood and snot, the exploding-diner sequence in Monty Python's The Meaning of Life is a paradigm of delicacy and restraint ... The plot of the film is ostentatiously irrelevant, a thin excuse for a series of set pieces involving swearing, maiming, perversity and fluids.

Many of these are not only impressively unpleasant - eyes are burned, nipples suffer, testicles go through torment - but are driven by underlying desires. Richie and Eddie's vicious fight in the hotel kitchen is the logical endpoint of all those displaced-gay slapstick spats in Laurel and Hardy films. An extended routine with rubber underpants offers a ballet of barely disguised buggery. Guest House Paradiso is, if nothing else, the film where the disavowed homoeroticism of the male comedy double act finally takes centre stage. At one point Richie and Eddie even blow smoke to each other through a hole in a connecting wall, which is either a homage

*to Jean Genet's classic Un Chant d'amour
(1950) or has been put there precisely to trap
pretentious queer intellectuals like me.*

*... What anyone who hadn't seen Bottom
would think is a mystery - those unaware
of Mayall and Edmondson's ongoing affair
with damaging each other might see only a
curious hybrid of Fawlty Towers and Ren and
Stimpy or be left wondering why educated
Englishmen never seem to tire of puke and
poo.'*

(ANDY MEDHURST, SIGHT AND SOUND, JANUARY 2000)

Guff

I vacillated for a long time about whether to include *Guest House Paradiso* in this guide. In all of their interviews at the time promoting the film, Rik and Ade kept saying it wasn't a *Bottom* movie. They then joked about how they've played the same characters for twenty-five years.

But just as Rick and Vyvyan wouldn't have grown up to be Richie and Eddie (they would have ended up in senior management at the BBC, and a well-respected surgeon), equally Richie Rich is no Dangerous Brother.

Guest House Paradiso <u>isn't</u> a *Bottom* movie, no matter what it might say on the DVD box.

Not least, because in their universe, Richie and Eddie are still trapped on Hooligan's Island.

Twat is fastidious, isn't desperate to be liked, nor

does he crave attention (he's rather handsome too), and Eddie is less intelligent, less cynical, less world-weary, less practical, and much more subservient to Twat (he loses all the fights).

The opening on the motorbike is nicely cinematic – there's a lot of beautiful shots in this movie. It's lit well too, and the sets are marvellous, invoking a rotten past in a different way to the *Bottom* set, with less filth, but lived in and out of date nonetheless.

For all these reasons, if you watch it expecting a *Bottom* movie, it will feel wrong – it's a much better experience when set apart from the sitcom. That said, what it gains from the big screen, it loses from a lack of studio audience. I enjoy hearing laughter in a sitcom, and the lack of it here throws the timing askew. The pauses for laughter are timed for a cinema audience, not for home viewing. Rik said on the *Film Buff* show that 'the only thing we haven't got is the intercourse with the audience.'

The kitchen fight is remarkably good, and it's fun to see the slapstick in a more elaborate way than we're used to. And the swing on the cliff edge is a fantastic visual gag.

When Gina touches Twat on the cheek, his reaction is understated and incredibly telling. It's a marvellous moment from Rik actually.

And just to hammer it home that this isn't *Bottom*, our main characters get to have a happy ending.

All in all, if you're expecting a *Bottom* movie, it just

doesn't work that way – but it works much, much better as a stand alone film from Rik and Ade. It owes just as much to *Dirty Movie* and *Mr Jolly Lives Next Door* as it does to *Bottom*.

Shot at Ealing Studios, and on location on the Isle Of Wight.

In an interview with the *Sunday Mirror* on 14th December 1997, Rik reveals that he's been writing a screenplay with Ade: 'We're convinced they want more *Bottom*. So we're sure the time is right for a movie version. We wanted to get away from the confines of a domestic sitcom for a change. Because I have done EVERYTHING in that kitchen. There's nothing left to hit Ade with. It's been very liberating writing for a film. You can do so much more stuff like plane crashes and explosions. Ade always says no-one does what we do.'

On Triple J Radio in Australia, Ade revealed that they were working on a second movie, which featured a king-fu scene. Rik also mentions The Larder, a file on Ade's computer that holds all their unused joke ideas.

Ade revised the script down from three and a half hours whilst Rik recovered in hospital after his quad bike accident.

Twat is reading *A History Of Wartime Underwear*.

Eddie has hand made a sign for the Honeymoon

Suet.

Eddie breaks the fourth wall, giving a look to camera as he pees from the motorbike, a few times during the kitchen fight, when Gina suggests she can trust him, and when he warns Gino about the PG rating he speaks to camera, and again when Gino gives him money. He makes a worried face down the barrel when he learns about the radioactive fish.

The dining room has been crudely divided in two by a wooden wall that cuts the fireplace in half.

That noise the swinging kitchen door makes is a reference to a similar door in *Les Vacances De Monsieur Hulot*, Jacques Tati's 1953 film. It's one of Rik's favourite films.

A Grenada poster is on the wall of the office.

There's a nice shot of Twat, leaning against the kitchen wall, framed so that two small flowers sit exactly over his nipples.

On the reverse of the Hotel Manager sign on the desk it says 'Another Bloody Customer'.

A painting on the stairs shows Rik (or Richie's ancestor) with a handlebar moustache, wearing britches, and leaning against a Union Flag draped over something. Another seems to show him as Christ on the shore having just walked on water.

Gina's middle name is Tortellini.

As the credits roll, we hear the Bonzo Dog Doo-Dah Band's *Jazz, Delicious Hot, Disgusting Cold*, which Rik and Ade acknowledge is a nod to the film *Sir Henry At Rawlinson End*.

BOTTOM 2001: AN ARSE ODDITY

Written by Adrian Edmondson and Rik Mayall
Produced by Emma Pitcher, Helen
Parker and Phil McIntyre
Directed by Dewi Humphreys
Presented by Phil McIntyre

Duration
1h27m

Tour Dates (all 2001)
Monday 17 September – Sunderland Empire
Wednesday 19 September – Newcastle City Hall
Thursday 20 September – Llandudno
North Wales Theatre
Friday 21 September – Southport Theatre
Saturday 22 September – Scarborough
Futurist Theatre
Monday 24 – Wednesday 26 September
– Southend Cliffs Pavilion
Thursday 27 September – York Barbican
Monday 1 October – Wolverhampton Civic Hall
Friday 5 October – Blackburn King George's Hall
Monday 8 October – Nottingham Royal Centre

Friday 12 – Saturday 13 October
– Liverpool Royal Court
Monday 15 October – Sheffield City Hall
Friday 19 October – Hull City Hall
Sunday 21 October Brighton Centre
Monday 22 October – Croydon Fairfield Halls
Tuesday 23 October – Watford Colosseum
Wednesday 24 October – Bristol Colston Hall
Thursday 25 October – Cardiff CIA
Saturday 27 October – Birmingham NIA
Monday 29 October – Manchester Apollo
Saturday 3 November – Dublin The Point
Sunday 4 November – Belfast Odyssey Arena
Monday 5 November – Blackpool Opera House
Wednesday 7 November Edinburgh Playhouse
Thursday 8 November – Glasgow
Clyde Auditorium
Sunday 11 November – Stoke-on-
Trent Regent Theatre
Monday 12 November – Portsmouth Guildhall
Tuesday 13 November – Plymouth Pavilions
Thursday 15 November Oxford Apollo
Monday 19 – Tuesday 20 November
– Leeds Grand Theatre
Monday 26 – Tuesday 27 November
– Ipswich Regent
Wednesday 28 November – Hammersmith Apollo
Friday 30 November – Bournemouth BIC

Recording Dates
Monday 8th October 2001 at the
Nottingham Royal Concert Hall

Monday 19th November 2001

"Comedy's wildest cult heroes" The Mirror

Bottom Live 4 finds Rik Mayall and Adrian Edmondson bravely and boldly poking their dirty bits into the start of new millennium. Armed only with an endless stream of knobgags, gallons of banana and raisin ouzo and the funniest, most outrageous stage show ever invented.

Filmed during the sell-out 2001 tour we find Richie and Eddie where we left them – stuck on a Pacific island and still the saddest pair of no-hope losers the world has known. Getting by on bone-crunching nastiness and violently successful accidents the hapless duo encounter an exploding parrot, experiment with chainsaw pant removal and indulge in a bout of enthusiastic pig worrying. It also looks like they manage to escape the island only for everything to become unhinged!

Bottom Live 2001, is explosively insane and unfettered by any morals whatsoever – disgusting, degrading vicious and so bloody funny you will laugh your bollocks off! (or tits if you're a girl)

"Their energy is something else ... incessant jokes about rear ends, dangly bits and flatulence have a delirious effect" Daily Mail

Cast
Richie – Rik Mayall
Eddie – Adrian Edmondson

Synopsis

Still stranded on Hooligan's Island, Eddie has been gambling in the jungle for the last three days, and Richie is stuck in a tight pair of pants. Eddie returns and helps him remove them, just as Dave, Richie's parrot, has a heart attack. After a failed attempt at revival, they bury him in a grave that Eddie has already dug for Richie.

To mourn their loss, they toast Dave at Eddie's bar, but boredom provokes a fight that Richie loses – leaving him to beg for the sweet release of death.

His prayer is answered, and he feels a sharp pain in his chest, but Eddie says that's just the tight pants. The second act begins in a strange, empty dome, with a giant button that says 'do not press'. They can't remember how they got here.

Guff

Richie and Eddie appear to have moved to a different location on the island, and God knows, and I don't want to know, how they survived the explosion. The convention of beginning with an unexplained mystery continues, with Eddie missing for the last three days – though he quickly arrives, via a swinging vine again, and this time in a French Legionnaires hat.

We've seen throughout his career that Rik keeps returning to the Nottingham Royal Concert Hall, and I can see why – it's a marvellous venue.

Eddie talking about a Playstation is remarkably incongruous. He's more of a darts or bar billiards man, surely?

There's an actual magic trick going on when Dave explodes – and it's done really well.

Eddie has finally had enough, and has been planning to murder Richie, probably because the alcohol is no longer blocking out his existence. And once more Richie reaches his bottom, and begs for death.

The first half of this show is always much better than I remember it being, and it could easily be an episode of the sitcom, in the flat. A wake, with just the two of them, descending into the exact fight that Eddie describes.

Act Two begins, and we have no idea where we are, with Richie and Eddie back in their normal clothes. It all gets a bit meta. Not just with the references to Rik and Ade, but the idea that they're stuck in this void, always ending up exactly where they started (a rather apt sitcom metaphor). This act is probably their most Beckettian – except maybe the pants song.

Looking at the tour dates, and noting the distinct lack of plot and shorter duration, I do wonder if there were some last minute changes to this play because of 9/11.

The title is of course a play on *2001: A Space Odyssey*.

Pants was written by Adrian Edmondson, Rik Mayall, Simon Brint, Peter Chill and Mark Johns.

Rik injured Adrian during a stunt at one performance, and the show had to be stopped while Ade went to hospital for stitches.

The sitcom that Richie says Spudgun starred in is *Lee Evans: So What Now.*

Richie mentions Rik's quad bike accident.

On Sunday 29th September 2002, Rik and Ade appeared on stage in *The Peter Cook Posthumous Tribute Show* at The Prince Of Wales Theatre in London. They performed an adapted version of the beginning of *Arse Oddity's* second act, and added their unique take on some classic sketches, including Rik's marvellous impressions of Cook, and also Derek and Clive.

One of the rock formations resembles someone naked bending over and showing the audience their arse. Another looks like a clam shell.

This time we get to see Edie's Bra.

Richie was once in the Hammersmith Territorial Army.

Unseen character Aunty Marjorie was at little

Torquille's christening.

BOTTOM LIVE 2003: WEAPONS GRADE Y-FRONTS TOUR

Written by Adrian Edmondson and Rik Mayall
Produced by Helen Parker and Phil McIntyre
Directed by Dewi Humphreys
Presented by Phil McIntyre

Duration
1h33m

Tour Dates (all 2003)
Friday 3 October – Glasgow Clyde Auditorium
Monday 6 – Tuesday 7 October
– Plymouth Pavilions
Wednesday 8 October – Portsmouth Guildhall
Friday 10 October – Bournemouth BIC
Sunday 12 – Monday 13 October –
Croydon Fairfield Halls
Wednesday 15 – Saturday 18 –
Nottingham Royal Centre
Monday 20 – Friday 24 October –

Leeds Grand Opera House
Saturday 25 October – Cardiff CIA
Sunday 26 October – Watford Colosseum
Tuesday 28 – Thursday 30 October
– Southend Cliffs Pavilion
Friday 31 October – Brighton Brighton Centre
Monday 3 November – Manchester Carling Apollo
Tuesday 4 – Wednesday 5 November
– Sheffield City Hall
Thursday 6 November –
Wolverhampton Civic Hall
Friday 7 November – Sunderland Empire
Saturday 8 November – Manchester Carling Apollo
Sunday 9 November – Ipswich Regent Theatre
Tuesday 11 November – Newcastle City Hall
Wednesday 12 November – Blackburn
King George's Hall
Friday 14 November – Llandudno
Theatre For North Wales
Saturday 15 November – Blackpool Opera House
Sunday 16 – Monday 17 November
– Oxford New Theatre
Wednesday 19 – Friday 21 November
– Bristol Hippodrome
Saturday 22 – Sunday 23 November –
Birmingham Academy at the NIA
Tuesday 25 – Wednesday 26 November
– Liverpool Empire Theatre
Thursday 27 – Saturday 29 November*
– Hammersmith Carling Apollo
Monday 1 – Tuesday 2 December –

Leicester De Montfort Hall
Friday 5 December – Dublin The Point
Saturday 6 December – Belfast Odyssey Arena
Monday 8 – Tuesday 9 December –
Ipswich Regent Theatre
Wednesday 10 December – Newcastle City Hall
Thursday 11 December –
Wolverhampton Civic Hall
(*an extra date was added here on 30th November)

Recording Dates
Tuesday 28th – Thursday 30th October 2003
at Cliffs Pavilion Southend-on-Sea

Original Release Dates
Monday 24th November 2003

DVD Back Matter

'Filthy slapstick from a pair of comedy virtuosos' Daily Express

This year's Bottom Live 5 is a terrifying, brain shreddingly deafening, rib-splintering, (technically illegal), insanely explosive live show. It's like Full Metal Jacket meets Apocalypse Now … in the toilet.

Rik and Ade of course star as the criminally insane no-hopers Richie and Eddie, who plan to save the world (and possibly destroy it trying) from a conflict much bigger than a mere Gulf War; the fight between good and underpants. Eddie has invented a time travelling toilet to help them along the way, but he's not feeling himself. If only he wouldn't get locked in it … He has all the weaponry, but is too stupid to use it, whilst Richie thinks it's all a pleasant social event – he's quite looking forward to feeling the sand between his toes. Rik says, 'You better bring some spare underwear! This time, it's death and destruction all the way. This is the big one.' Recorded at Southend's Cliffs Pavilion, Bottom: Weapons Grade Y-Fronts offers fans all the belching, vulgarities and knock-a-bout laughs they have come to expect from these two psychopaths.

'Their incessant jokes about rear ends, dangly bits and flatulence have a cumulative, delirious effect on the audience'
Daily Mail

Cast
Richie – Rik Mayall
Eddie – Adrian Edmondson

Synopsis

Having escaped Hooligan's Island, Richie and Eddie find themselves back at the flat in Hammersmith. And Eddie is back to his old ways, locking himself in his room for the past fifteen days, and Richie is getting fed up. So he barges in, and finds a bevy of inventions which Eddie has plagiarised from Richie's dead uncle Peregrine. One of the inventions is an elixir of life, which

Richie hurriedly drinks, only to find that it's actually poison. Eddie uses his time machine to stop this happening, and they realise they can travel in time to avoid the queue at the bar during the interval.

Three and a half years later, and they still haven't managed to locate the bar. They travel further and further back in time, and arrive at the start of the universe, where they discover the meaning of existence.

Reviews

'Rik Mayall and Adrian Edmondson have both enjoyed previous success, most memorably in The Young Ones. Bottom is another madcap anarchic sitcom-style show featuring their grotesquely puerile comic creations, Richie Richard and Eddie Hitler.

This, a live spin-off from the 1990s' BBC series, certainly does good box office, which is evident in a nearly full Point Depot, but when it comes to innovative and original comedy it's a hopeless waste of time. This is toilet humour at its most literal, featuring a time-travelling toilet called the Turdis. The fact that this was one of the best-received gags proves just how unfunny Mayall and Edmondson's Bottom creations are.

They press ahead with a highly annoying

blend of slapstick, crudity, dreadful jokes and awful stage Oirish accents in an abortive attempt to win over the locals. The only contemporary reference is a cringe-worthy Michael Jackson mention, which at this stage is about as funny as getting your mobile nicked.

This travesty was fully titled as Bottom: Weapons Grade Y-Fronts Tour, an atrocious sequel to Bottom: An Arse Odyssey (sic) which did the rounds in 2001. Just how this pair gets away with milking the boring existence of two repulsive bachelors is completely beyond me. They obviously do appeal to more than just a few, but it's striking how muted the reaction is in the seats surrounding me. Gentle ripples of laughter and occasional applause comes from the more up-for-it crowd downstairs, but it's a far cry from the euphoric guffawing a genuinely talented act would induce.

What's worse is that as a live experience, this is like watching a sitcom re-created in a massive arena. Pay a fraction of the ticket price to see any emergent stand-up in a comedy club and one is guaranteed far more entertainment. If you're a comic genius of the calibre of Billy Connolly or Eddie Izzard, playing the enormodromes is a logical progression. But this badly executed version of a TV show should have stayed on the small screen where it belongs.'

(EAMON SWEENEY, IRISH INDEPENDENT, 12TH DECEMBER 2003)

Guff

We open on just the set – which is interestingly cartoonish and abstract. I like how the colour palette suggests a toilet and a laboratory all at once. They have a rather large bathroom nowadays. Wonder if this is a different flat than before. Either way, it's nice that they're back home. Eddie always gets to make a dramatic entrance, and this one is probably the best.

And just to smash home a point with a frying pan, their first fight ensues the moment that Richie asks Eddie to imagine he's Tony Blair. The hope of new Labour has gone for these characters, which is why they've been allowed to come home.

There's a tenuous metaphor to be strained in Richie really enjoying himself when sucked dry from the inside (not that he's just full of shit, either). Something about doffing the cap to our 'betters' …

This may be the first time we see Richie's actual bottom.

It's also a rare occasion when Richie addresses Eddie's alcoholism – the latter admitting it's his only means of escape, while the former laments that it's destroyed their friendship. So when the conversation gets too real, they resort to a pantomime of American drama. It's a genuine character moment, hidden in daftness.

This show finally confirms that Richie does actually come from aristocracy, or at least from a monied family that has a coat of arms. They've obviously fallen on harder times more recently, or even ostracised Richie. No wonder his sense of entitlement is in the stratosphere. It offers a strange contradiction; he's at once upper and lower class. Rent asunder from that unearned wealth, Richie is nobody, and has nothing to offer society aside from a hatred of the 'commoner', and an unhealthy obsession with breeding.

Act Two brings another void, and sees Richie and Eddie lost to time (how apt). It starts with a role reversal in a rather Dangerous Brothers–esque routine with dynamite, and moves into a reference to *Arse Oddity*. All before a crowd-pleasing *Young Ones* moment.

Eddie asking Richie why everyone hates him makes for an interesting point. We don't like Richie, we're not meant to like him, but somehow Rik makes him into someone we can identify with. In the same way that Alan B'Stard speaks to our darker sides, so does Richie. There's a lot of difficult truth to him that we don't like seeing reflected back at ourselves. We don't like him because he reminds us of aspects of our selves we don't like – narcissism, loneliness, etc – but we know him all too well, and it's hard to ignore him.

And so we leave Richie and Eddie for the last time,

stranded at the beginning of time, with only one another for company for the rest of eternity.

Nuggets

Richie claims that Rik's quad bike accident was caused by Eddie – something Eddie himself admitted during *Arse Oddity*.

A crack in the tiling on the wall is in the shape of a naked woman sticking out her bottom.

There's a mention of the Lamb And Flag, the first for a long time now.

Richie has a tattoo of Ethel Cardew's name and phone number on his penis.

A few unseen relatives of Richie's, including Great Uncle Peregrine, Aunty Marjorie, and Great Great Uncle Withenthrop.

BACK

As we've seen over and over again, *Bottom* was lauded and dismissed (often by the same person at different time) as lavatorial. As slapstick. As boorish. As childish. As laddish. It was rarely, if ever, examined in much more depth than that. But *Bottom* and *The Young Ones* provide complimentary bookends to a more than a decade of divisive and contentious Tory rule. Rooted in a timeless parody of Little England, it examined and pilloried a status quo that kept people down and taught them to deflect the blame elsewhere.

For all the allusions we like to draw to Hancock, Beckett, *Steptoe and Son*, Laurel And Hardy, and Jacques Tati, underneath it all lies a seething socio-political satire.

And it's the show's very deliberate timelessness that means it still feels relevant today.

Perhaps that's why I was taken aback when my friend in school the next day dismissed it as a 'bit rude', because there was so much more to it then, and there's still so much more to it now.

That's it.

Fuck off.

www.ingramcontent.com/pod-product-compliance
Lightning Source LLC
Chambersburg PA
CBHW020317160726
47992CB00004B/1577